manifesto *for* new times
a strategy for the 1990s

manifesto
for new times
a strategy for the 1990s

the Communist Party

London

the **Communist Party**
16 St John Street
London EC1M 4AY

First published 1990

© the Communist Party of Great Britain, 1990

Published in association with Lawrence & Wishart Ltd, London.
Cover and text design by Jan Brown Designs, London.
Photoset in North Wales by
Derek Doyle & Associates, Mold, Clwyd.
Printed and bound by Dotesios Printers Ltd,
Trowbridge, Wiltshire.

contents

foreword 7

introduction 9

socialism: towards a fuller way of life 11
Humanitarian Socialism
An Outline
Democracy
Interdependence

the new times 18
A World in Metamorphosis
The Settlements: Sites of Struggles
The Period of Turbulence
The New Times

thatcherism 27
Regressive Radicalism
Class Politics
Thatcherism and the State

the opposition to thatcherism 33
Economic Restructuring and Trade Unions
Economic Ideology
Inequality
Authoritarianism
Scotland: a Case Study of Resistance
Nationalism and Internationalism
Ideology and Parties

a vision for the 1990s 42

a different kind of politics 46
Reconstructing the Social
The Failure of the Political Left
Paths to Renewal

contents

Defeating Thatcherism
Renewal

the communist party   57

sustainable development   62

between and beyond nations   66
Globalisation
New Global Challenges
The Break-up of the Superpower World
Europe
Response
Ireland

new times, new economy   74
Goals
Means
Local, National and International
Markets and Planning
Macro and Micro

the social society   85
State and Society
The Collective and the Individual
Experts and People
Needs and Efficiency
Housing
Childcare

political settlement   92

conclusion   96

foreword

Manifesto for New Times is an unusual document in several ways.

It was drafted before the political tidal wave that swept across Europe in 1989. Yet it is so firmly anchored in an underlying analysis of 'new times', and so committed to pluralism and democracy, that these revolutions which have shaken the world's political foundations validate rather than undermine the essential tenets of the Manifesto.

Although the document reflects the popular mood prior to the tenth anniversary of Mrs Thatcher's term in Downing Street and tends to be somewhat dismissive of the prospects for Labour, the basic argument remains centrally important: Thatcherism has been a reactionary modernising force to which socialists cannot respond simply by defending past gains and old demands. We must instead develop an alternative vision of the future that runs with the grain of the new times, that addresses itself to the contours of the new political, economic and social landscape.

We hope that the Manifesto, with its rich vision of a new politics, democratic renewal, citizenship, alliance and proportional representation, will serve as a welcome antidote for those who fear that Labour's new confidence heralds a return to the depressing and barren vista of the first-past-the-post system, the 'swingometer' of two-party politics, and the general cynicism of electoral politics.

The Manifesto is also a remarkably optimistic document. It recognised in uncompromising language the bankruptcy of 'actually existing' versions of socialism before they finally collapsed in Eastern Europe, and decisively rejected such discredited models for socialists in Britain. But far from abandoning the values of socialism – co-operation, collectivity, equal opportunity and social justice – the Manifesto argues that these values are increasingly relevant if we are to overcome the global problems of poverty and environmental damage.

The Manifesto's orientation to both the new times and a wider global perspective is essential to sustaining and renewing critical, democratic Marxism in Britain. It enables us to face honestly the corruption and authoritarianism perpetrated in Eastern Europe in the name of Communism, and to recognise that with the collapse of that edifice we are left with one foot in the rubble. Only by disentangling ourselves from the wreckage can we judge what remains of value from the tradition of Marxism in the twentieth century and reclaim that from the damage caused by Stalinism. This also necessitates a re-evaluation of Leninism. The *Manifesto* represents a serious attempt to modernise Marxism, which demands a fundamental reassessment of the relationship between class interest and the rights of the individual and of nature. Improving that relationship means embracing pluralism and drawing contributions from other traditions.

The wider vision of the *Manifesto* aims to reinforce the courage of socialists to make this honest reappraisal, and give them the heart to go on working for a revitalised democratic socialism. The new times present both challenges and opportunities for a progressive politics which will continue to strive to involve people in creating a better society – a society that is more humane than the dog-eat-dog values of contemporary capitalism.

These features of the *Manifesto* stem from the large numbers of people who creatively participated in its drafting – a process which involved extensive public discussion as well as wide-ranging debate within the Communist Party. This edition is published after amendment and adoption by the 41st Congress of the Communist Party in November 1989.

The Communist Party is now engaged in discussion about how to renew its tradition in order to give most effective expression in everyday life to the politics envisaged in the *Manifesto*. If you want to take part in this process, please write to me at this address.

Nina Temple
Secretary, the Communist Party
16 St John Street
London EC1M 4AY

introduction

This document is about how Britain can make progress in the 1990s. It is about how people can face the stark realities of environmental destruction and open up possibilities for progressive change, creating a popular politics for a new era. After a decade in which Thatcherism has been the dominant political force in British politics, this document is intended to offer ideas, hope and purpose to all who want to see Britain develop in a more democratic, sustainable, egalitarian and open way.

Progressive change in the 1990s is the essential first step towards putting socialism back on to the political agenda. The Communist Party is seeking to be part of a force in Britain which can create a new, popular political atmosphere, where we can talk with confidence about a shared vision of a socialist future.

Thatcherism is the most immediate obstacle blocking the way to change. But Thatcherism will only be defeated electorally if it is also defeated politically and ideologically. A movement to defeat Thatcherism must be underpinned by a common vision: of a society which moves to the rhythm of a popular humanism rather than a popular capitalism. That vision will be generated by popular aspirations for progressive change, aspirations which will emerge from people's fears, concerns and ambitions as they face the 1990s. To express those aspirations is the greatest challenge and opportunity for the Left and progressive forces.

Society is entering a distinctive phase of development, which we call 'new times'. Production, power and politics are becoming global in their sweep. Technology is transforming how people work. Society is becoming more divided – division which has been deepened systematically under Thatcherism – with about one third of people trapped on or below the poverty line, and the majority two thirds experiencing relative material prosperity. Women's employment is rising to more than 50 per cent of the workforce. Attachments to the common identity bred by class are weakening.

Society is going through an epochal change. This restructuring requires an equally fundamental rethinking of our politics. We should not be fearful of this change – rather, we should embrace it. The crucial political question at the heart of the new times is: on whose terms will the new era be moulded? The new times bring new threats, but they are also creating possibilities. Powerful social currents are emerging on each of the central issues facing society, which offer an alternative democratic, humane, yet modernising, path.

The green movement responds to the environmental crisis with a sweeping challenge to current economic priorities, be they global or personal. Internationalisation has found its echo in the campaigns and movements over aid and disarmament, which express a new popular international humanism. There is mounting moral and political opposition to the savage inequalities and authoritarianism of Thatcherism's conservative modernisation. The growth of women's employment is matched by feminism's agenda to make women the authors of their lives. Nationalism presents a fundamental challenge to the character of the British state, insisting that it be remade democratically. The sweeping-away of Stalinist regimes in Eastern Europe and the moves towards plural democracy in the Soviet Union provide unprecedented opportunities for internationalist progressive political thinking.

After ten years of Thatcherism there is a new mood, a common sense murmuring in society. Partly founded on existing collective values which have resisted Thatcherite individualism, this mood speaks of a popular humanism rather than popular capitalism, a progressive internationalism rather than British-bulldog nationalism, citizenship rather than enterprise culture, democratic individualism rather than the consumerism and authoritarianism of Thatcherism. The development and common purpose of these new times aspirations and values are the key to progressive advance in Britain in the 1990s.

That advance is not automatic. During ten years of Thatcherism the new times have been shaped by radical right-wing forces. The damage done – to the economy, to social provision and to the labour and progressive movement – will not be easily reversed. To move beyond defensiveness, we now need some clear and coherent ideas about a different future for Britain.

It is with that aim in mind that the Communist Party publishes this document, to stimulate creative, confident, purposeful political debate and action: a progressive politics which is on the move into the new times.

socialism:
towards a fuller way of life

We want to see a country in which women can go about their lives without fear of attack, where the colour of someone's skin is not a virtual guarantee of unemployment or a low-paid job, where work – whether social, productive or domestic – would be properly valued and rewarded. A society in which children are freed from abuse and are respected as human beings, a society which values and cares for its older citizens.

We want a modernising society, which uses science and technology to bequeath clear seas and fresh air to future generations. A society where by limiting our demands on nature and sharing resources between all peoples we can overcome the divide between First and Third Worlds. We want a society in which people have the power and resources to make and remake their own lives.

This is our vision of socialism. Against its standards of democracy, justice, equality, sustainable development, compassion and care our capitalist society does miserably badly.

This vision is about leaving behind a capitalist society marked by authoritarianism, exploitation, an ever-present threat of war, vast inequalities in wealth and power, and the despoliation of nature.

This does not mean people will suddenly become co-operative, honest, noble, virtuous, responsible and unselfish, where once they might have been competitive, cynical, grasping, vain, self-seeking and harsh. But it does mean people will live without the systematic threat of coercion and humiliation, oppression and exploitation.

Humanitarian Socialism

a socialist society would be committed to providing equal life chances to all, regardless of background, gender or race. It would be founded on socialist citizenship, embracing rights to education throughout life, a decent income and involvement in decision-making.

Socialist citizenship would widen and deepen the quality of life. It would enhance the natural environment through the kind of development which did not constantly deplete natural resources. It would enhance the economic environment through investment in skills, science and technology, and the social environment, through mutual support for child-rearing, education and health.

A socialist society would value diverse cultural and artistic projects, and would give practical support and encouragement to people to express themselves through art-forms as an important realisation of individual potential.

Socialist citizenship would offer more than a package of benefits. It would be founded upon people's energy and confidence to take personal responsibility, to be agents of social change, to shoulder obligations to society, to give support to others, as well as to claim their individual rights.

But individuality must be matched by a sense of community. The rights and needs we share in common are a prerequisite for people to have an equal chance to satisfy their individual aspirations. Socialist citizenship would be about people participating in a community together.

That sense of community and common good cannot be monolithic. It must be flexible and open to change. And it will be greatly enhanced when people have the resources they need and deserve to develop their lives as members of society. The collective character of socialism should be about its capacity to address the multiple and highly diverse ways in which people wish to develop their lives.

Popular, democratic control of production, work and consumption is needed for people to develop to the full their capacity for creativity, thought and pleasure. That means ending the gross inequalities in economic and social power of capitalism.

The oppression of racism must be overcome in all areas of

society. Male power, which limits women's potential for free thought and action, must be successfully challenged, and women's right to choose whether or not to have children positively supported. A climate must be created in which people can make free choices about their sexuality and living patterns, free from the oppressive belief that equates heterosexuality with normality.

Socialism will be created by myriad movements through a long, uneven struggle to change society. These movements will come from different starting points, with different objectives. But already they are beginning to find common purpose. Socialist and communist ideas and struggles share much with the green movement, feminists, community groups, internationalists, radical liberals, and religious groups: for all are about creating a more democratic, humanitarian society.

What is distinctive about our vision is that we believe economic and political power, in this country and internationally, will have to be transformed to create a more humanitarian society. This is not just desirable. It will be necessary if the waste of capitalism is to be brought to an end. We believe this change can be brought about by people through political struggle.

An Outline

the detailed organisation of socialist society, its laws and institutions, will be decided by the generations which make and remake socialism in their time. There is no blueprint ready for inspection. But for most of this century the main version of 'socialism' on offer has been that model of society which emerged in the aftermath of the Russian Revolution.

The Russian Revolution of 1917 set off a wave of socialist liberation struggles throughout the world, ushering in a historic phase in world development. The ensuing change in the balance of world forces was to prove crucial to ending colonialism and defeating Fascism. Nor should we underestimate the social and economic achievements that followed.

But the revolution also bequeathed a tarnished socialism, in which the individual and civil society were subordinated to the state and the party. Those regimes sought to justify their authoritarian and repressive nature by developing a rigid and dogmatic ideology which borrowed the language of Marxism, while distorting its essence.

Gorbachev's perestroika has confronted this legacy, and aims to renovate completely Soviet society. It is creating the first opportunity in a generation for communists and socialists across the world to talk the same language, to heal the disastrous rifts and estrangements caused by Stalinism, the cold war and later the period of stagnation under Brezhnev. The creative risks Gorbachev has taken with the meaning of socialism should be taken up by socialists in the West as part of a worldwide process of radical renewal.

Although we cannot and should not offer a blueprint, we can outline the main elements of a future humanistic, socialist society.

It would be founded upon a sustainable, socialised economy, which would serve people's needs rather than the imperative of profit or the demands of central planners. Economic development would sustain the social and ecological environment with cities and towns built for people rather than cars or capital; healthy, safe workplaces; forms of production, trade and consumption which do not foul our air, sea and land.

The concept of employment itself would encompass a far wider range of productive human labour and activity than at present, properly and fairly rewarded. Full employment is an essential aim of any dignified socialist society. And people's work should serve their individual needs and aspirations as well as the collective needs of society.

But socialism is not an enormous economic almshouse. The domestic and international market will play a role, as will professional, enterprising management. With democratic planning setting the strategic aims of economic development, the market would encourage flexibility, diversity and dynamism. What matters is the social interests which determine how the tools of market and plan are to be used.

For the socialist transformation of society to succeed, the concentrations of power that prevail in a capitalist economy would have to be broken down, and key sectors of the economy held in social ownership. But power would not be reconcentrated in the hands of the state. Ownership would be democratically controlled and participation devolved in diverse forms through society, not only from rich to poor, but also from men to women and white to black.

Along with this would go democratic decision-making within businesses and a range of democratic local controls, national laws and international regulations covering large and transnational businesses.

Socialist modernisation would not abolish scarcity though, and social and economic conflicts would remain. A socialist society could not legislate hard choices out of existence – but it would confront them in a different way. Democratic decision-making in all areas of society would be essential, involving a thorough democratisation of the state, which is so central to the struggle for a successful development of socialist society.

Democracy

a self-managing society will require an open political system, with power dispersed away from the centre and a culture in which the old boundaries between public and private, personal and political are transcended. Since socialism is about the problem of power and powerlessness, then socialist strategy must engage everywhere in society with power and powerlessness, in all its dimensions.

This will include multi-party democracy; proportional representation; transformed local and regional councils; parliaments for Scotland, Wales and England; democratic bodies responsible for strategic policy on housing, health, education and the environment; and accountability of all public bodies, including the vast civil service which sustains the workings of the state. It will require strong autonomous movements and organisations in society to represent the plurality of social groups and concerns – for instance, independent trade unions, collective organisations for black people, women, lesbians and gay men, consumers, writers and artists.

The oppressive and unequal relations between women and men, black and white, children and adults, able-bodied and disabled and those who choose different sexualities, mean that existing power relationships in the home and in our culture need to be dismantled and democratised just as much as power in the public politics of institutions and in economic organisations and activities.

It would be a much more equal society, with material resources and services distributed according to need, to make a decent life a possibility for everyone. It would be committed to publicly financed health care and a frontal assault on national, ethnic, gender and class differences in mortality and illness. It would guarantee equal access to public education through life. It would be a fair, tolerant but secular society. Religious differences would be respected but not elevated into positions of power or control over people's lives.

A much more equal society does not mean everyone will be treated the same. People have different needs and aspirations. Minorities must be protected, with rights tailored to suit their particular needs.

There would still be differentials in material rewards and incentives, for unpleasant, unsocial jobs, and for special skills. But differentials would have to be limited, within ranges which were openly debated and democratically agreed, based on much wider definitions of people's work and contributions, whether through paid work or domestic responsibilities and caring services.

Interdependence

Socialism cannot be isolated from a world which is becoming more integrated, through global trade, mass communication, and the shared threat of nuclear incineration, radioactive pollution and ecological catastrophe. Socialism in Britain will vitally depend on moves to create a more progressive international political framework. The world is our common home. We have to take responsibility for it together.

The protection of the environment, conservation of resources, resolving the debt crisis and raising the living standards of the majority of the world's population means facing up to the idea of 'sustainable development': ie, development within the framework of safeguarding the planet and its resources. And that will require big changes in the world economy, to overcome the North/South gap which drains resources and wealth from the poorest countries.

A socialist Britain would play a progressive world role:

pressing the United Nations to expand its influence, urging the creation of new international institutions to regulate the economy and helping create a new international economic order. Britain would be committed to disarmament, the peaceful resolution of conflict, international human rights and the elimination of poverty. Socialism cannot be made in Britain on the backs of the people in the developing world. Our conception of the future, our perspective of socialism, has to be global. No country can escape from global problems. The crucial division today is between those who recognise the need to tackle the global issues, and those who persist in old attitudes to the arms race and international relations, including the unequal division of the world's wealth.

It is in this sense that universal human values have primacy over class divisions. However, the principles that need to prevail in the new internationalism of an interdependent world are those that spring from socialist traditions, from progressive religious outlooks and humanism, which conflict with the motivating principles of capitalism. This is the basis for a new definition of socialism suited to new times.

the new times

A World in Metamorphosis

as we enter the 1990s Britain will be a capitalist society, riven with enormous inequalities in income, wealth and power. But it will be a different kind of capitalist society from the 1930s or 1950s. International capitalism is entering a distinctive phase of development from that which has governed our lives and shaped our world over the past 45 years.

Three key developments laid the foundations for postwar British society. Firstly, the depression of the 1930s led industry to shift from 19th-century production methods based on coal and steam, to the new technologies based on electricity, oil and petrol. At Ford's Dagenham plant, opened in 1931, the company introduced the mass production techniques – known as 'Fordism' – which were to have a sweeping impact on the rest of industry. They left an indelible mark on the economy, workers, consumers and social life. These new methods were propelled by a concentration of ownership, sometimes through traditional family ownership, increasingly through a more dominant role by corporate bodies, with a wave of mergers and acquisitions, which created now familiar household names like ICI and GEC.

The second factor was the economic, social and political upheaval of the struggles against unemployment and Fascism in the 1930s, which culminated during the second world war. Social aspirations, together with working-class and democratic pressure bred by the war, propelled the Labour Party into power with a wide-ranging reform programme – nationalisation, the creation of the National Health Service, the expansion of public education, an enormous council house building programme, the introduction of a system of welfare benefits, and perhaps above all, a commitment to maintain full employment through Keynesian economic policies.

The third factor was the postwar disintegration of Britain's colonial empire and successful anti-colonial conflicts in many developing countries. Attempts at first to resist this process and later to adapt to it had profound consequences for our economic position and changing social composition.

The postwar settlement created an institutional and political framework to meet both companies' demands for profitable markets and popular desires for rising living standards. It was made up of several component 'settlements', which set the parameters and became focal points for conflict and arenas of struggle.

The Settlements: Sites of Struggle

The economic core was an *industrial settlement*. Large manufacturing factories sucked in armies of mainly semi-skilled labour to work in a strictly regulated division of labour on assembly lines, pumping out standardised products. The large manufacturing plants, taking up the mass production methods of Fordism, were the leading edge of economic development, capitalist profitability and accumulation. They also became the leading edge for industrial struggle between increasingly well organised unions and employers over productivity and pay.

This industrial settlement was at the heart of a wider *economic settlement*. Full employment gave the labour movement considerable strength in collective bargaining. It also meant companies could profit from a growing, protected national market. The full productivity gains of standardised, mass production could only be unleashed with a mass consumer market created by full employment and rising living standards. The balance between wages and public spending on the one hand, and the rate of profits and taxation on the other, was in continual conflict. But the power of big business was never seriously weakened.

The economic settlement was entwined with a *social settlement*. The establishment of the NHS represented an enormous advance, though weakened from the outset by the deal struck with the consultants, private drug companies and private practice. There were big advances in public education through the development of comprehensive education in schools from the 1960s and greater access to higher education, but a significant private education sector remained. Televisions, fridges, vacuum cleaners and cars transformed consumption and domestic work, creating the affluence of the postwar years. The expansion of public services, from broadcasting to the NHS, created a new politics of mass public consumption. Public sector, white-collar service work expanded, and with it public sector unionism and industrial struggle within the state, while both employees and users of the public services were excluded from any real involvement in decision-making within them.

Running through all these developments was an unstable, contested and conservative *gender settlement* of relations between men and women. Women had filled the labour market during the war, struggling for adequate nursery provision and against union agreements which ensured their employment was temporary.

After the war, however, the patriarchal settlement between capital and labour was re-established. Women were immediately expelled from the labour market. When they subsequently re-entered, it was in the context of a new and rigid sexual division of labour in which women, more than ever, moved between paid and unpaid labour, unmatched by any transformation in men's relation to children, women, or domesticity.

To women's new postwar identity was added another: they became, *par excellence*, the focus of consumption. It was women who used the newly available domestic appliances. Their role as 'mothers' was promoted through ideological and cultural developments, including new popular theories of child development. And it was women, as recipients of child benefit, who became the vital link between state welfare and the family budget.

Society was also marked by an oppressive *racial settlement* – a legacy of Britain's spent imperial role – the assertion of white privilege and power against Caribbean and Asian immigrants. Encouraged into Britain's labour market in the 1950s and 60s, they were to face a widespread colour bar in jobs, homes and services. Black workers were abandoned to a racist culture which refused to make any accommodations to them. Most disastrously, a racist housing market confined black people largely to the bomb-damaged inner cities. Immigration rules were consistently racist, while discrimination was inscribed in all public practices from the labour market to the town hall, and from the 1950s onwards there was periodic growth in activity by and support for explicitly racist extremist political groups.

The massive industrial and urban growth rested upon an

implicit, exploitative *environmental settlement*. It was embedded in the industrialism of the big factory and the overpowering modernism of the tower block, and in pollution from cars, power stations and chemical plants.

Britain's economic growth had been highly uneven geographically. Many key mass production companies congregated within a core region stretching northwards from the Midlands, and on the outskirts of London. This imbalance promoted continual pressure for government policies to spread growth through regional policy. Under that *regional settlement*, workers and consumers were drawn to sprawling conurbations in which slums were replaced by modern, functional housing, corner shops were overtaken by supermarkets, and the north-south divide sharpened.

The postwar period was also defined by a *national settlement* in which the national interests of the people of Wales and Scotland were denied, producing for them an extra dimension of exploitation and deprivation.

The situation in Northern Ireland has constituted the most intractable problem facing all British governments. Partition, and the failure to recognise the Irish people's right to self-determination, has meant that as Britain faces the close of the century the crisis over Ireland, which it had at the start of it, continues.

Binding together all these different characteristics of postwar society was a *party political settlement*, commonly referred to as a 'political consensus', between the Labour Party and the Conservative Party. As the product of years of progressive struggle, this represented an enormous political advance over the prewar period. But it was a settlement which also served to limit economic and social advance, and which disappointed millions who aspired to more radical reforms in key areas. So it was mainly unprofitable and failing enterprises that were nationalised. Massive compensation charges and a requirement to provide cheap facilities for private industry left them recording heavy financial losses: then represented as a failure of socialist nationalisation.

Over the years then, the political settlement ossified. The radical energy of the Labour Party in 1945 had been largely dissipated 30 years later and the reforming zeal of the immediate postwar period slowly gave way to the miserable pragmatism of the Callaghan era.

Finally, Britain was one player in an *international settlement*. It was founded upon the industrial, economic and military power of the United States, the cold war arms race, the regulation of the international economy through the Bretton Woods currency system and the spreading neo-colonialism of US multinationals to Europe, Africa, Latin America and Asia.

Britain was already one of the most multinational economies in the West. In the face of independence struggles and the rapid disintegration of the British Empire it clung to its imperial legacy – which provided the manufacturing industry with protected markets – to disguise its weakness. And crucially, it tried to preserve its world role through nuclear weapons. Some of the most advanced sectors of the economy – electronics, new materials, fast computers, communications – have absorbed huge proportions of skilled, scientific and technical personnel and resources on military research and development. This was the source of one of the most potent contradictions of the postwar settlement: the combination of a highly internationalised economy and a xenophobic sense of self-importance which did not match the reality of Britain's decline.

The Period of Turbulence

In the 1970s those interlocking, contested settlements began to break apart, provoking a tumultuous crisis at the end of the decade. It was not accidental, but rather a structural crisis, created by long-term weaknesses of development. It disrupted not only the economic organisation and management of society, but also the social and political fabric itself.

The crisis of the 1970s provoked two fundamental developments which set the stage for Thatcherism, and which are shaping our times.

Firstly, there was a political struggle to galvanise rumbling discontents over the decaying postwar settlement and the failing Keynesian, social-democratic state. It was a struggle the labour and democratic movement lost.

While the Right in the labour movement pushed an increasingly autocratic, visionless agenda, the Left was trapped by a complacency that the movement's future was guaranteed by history. So although the Left participated in broad social movements – for instance, anti-nuclear campaigns – and although it developed new ideas such as the alternative economic strategy, it did not offer a popular, modernising perspective able to coalesce disenchantment with the postwar settlement behind a new phase of socialist development.

But there was a second, equally important factor at work: capitalism's search for a successor to the regime of accumulation developed in the 1930s. Multinational companies by the early 1980s were on the lookout for new production methods, to raise productivity and profitability in the face of intensifying international competition.

These large companies in search of a secure position within increasingly global markets, are the key forces reorganising the UK economy. It is their response to international competition that is driving crucial changes in workplace technology, the structure of industry, the ownership of companies, the location of investment and consumption patterns.

The New Times

If the postwar settlement was created by the confluence of the 1930s economic restructuring and the popular impetus for social-democratic reforms, the 1980s have been shaped by a different dual revolution: the confluence of Thatcherism's radical right-wing politics with an international wave of capitalist restructuring.

At the industrial heart of the new times will be a shift to information technology and microelectronics. The new technologies allow production to be more flexible, automated and integrated.

These changes are not confined to manufacturing. Banks and building societies are also using information technology to innovate new services and products. It is seeping into the public sector and local authorities.

Much of postwar capitalism reflected the mass production methods of Fordism. In the new times, the organisation of work is being transformed into 'post-Fordism'. This does not mean that mass production will disappear. Rather, it means that production and work is taking on more flexible, diverse, fragmentary forms, around flexible team-working within much smaller, more skilled workforces. Services will continue to provide the main source of new jobs, fuelling the continued rise of women's part-time employment which will be at the core of the 1990s economy. Post-Fordism does not describe the whole economy, but rather the leading edge of the most competitive, modernising companies.

Combined with persistent mass unemployment, these changes are creating deeper divisions in the workforce. There will be more professional, highly skilled technicians' jobs, but also more low-skilled, low-wage, low-technology jobs. The economy will be marked by divisions between core full-time workers in large companies and the growing number of part-timers in small sub-contractors, between those in employment and the long-term unemployed. The traditional bases for union organisation are declining.

This upheaval in the industrial and economic core of modern capitalism is one of the forces producing ever greater social fragmentation, diversity and polarisation.

Some forms of that polarisation are very savage. A very small and very rich minority have done extremely well and in general Britain is becoming a two-thirds/one-third society, with a growing gulf between the majority – itself highly differentiated – leading relatively comfortable lives, and the one third trapped in poverty.

There is a sharply growing contrast between the north with its high levels of unemployment and the south-east with its shortage of skilled labour. Yet the south groans under the strain of an inadequate transport system and unaffordable mortgages, offsetting much recent growth in personal prosperity.

The welfare state – underfunded and financially vulnerable since its inception – is increasingly ill-equipped to cope with high unemployment and the growth in the number of single-parent families who are faced with the continuing privatisation of childcare. At the same time the growth of women's employment may well undermine conservative gendered assumptions about the division of labour between paid work and domestic responsibilities.

The demographic time bomb is already beginning to have a

major impact on the labour market. The rapid increase in children and pensioners is mirroring a reduction in the proportion of the population of working age. Both ends of the demographic shift pose new challenges for the way society treats its different groups, politically, economically and culturally.

A new political map is taking shape in the 1990s. Its extremes will be the politics of race and the underclass in the inner city, and the growth of new industrial regions such as the M4 corridor, fostering growth towns like Swindon and Basingstoke. The labour movement is present in these towns, but its culture is not central to them, in the way that it was in Sheffield in the early part of the century or Coventry during the heyday of engineering.

The local politics of town and city has become a key site for conflict between international capital and the community. All cities, from Bridgend to Dundee and Skelmersdale, are in a bitter competitive search for foreign investment to attract an international growth sector to their industrial estates. The competition has been intensified by harsh and unequal government regional policy and the constraints on local authorities' abilities to plan economic development.

A vital part of this new political geography is the resurgence of nationalism in Scotland and Wales in response to Thatcherism's authoritarianism, and the disproportionate costs of restructuring they have borne. The next decade will also be shaped by the environmental crisis bequeathed by Fordism: from our congested, polluted conurbations and the impact of that classic postwar product – the car – to the global crisis of the greenhouse effect.

As for the postwar international settlement: the two-dimensional world of superpower conflict is giving way to a more complex set of international relations. Establishing Britain's position within a new international order will be a key political task of the coming decade.

The 1990s will see myriad political and social struggles. Thatcherism's attempt to facilitate a 'conservative modernisation' will create privatisation, polarisation, fragmentation, public squalor and authoritarianism. Its grip will only be broken by a progressive movement gathered around the aspirations bred by the new times. And on each of the central issues facing society there are powerful progressive forces developing. These movements do not necessarily share the same interests, nor have they automatic cause to unite. They are moods, currents and forces in society, whose discontent is as much with the postwar settlement as with Thatcherism's moulding of the new times. They could offer an alternative vision of modernisation which is as credible and potentially more popular than Thatcherism's.

thatcherism

In the last decade Thatcherism has set out to reshape society in the image of popular capitalism and enterprise culture. As such, it has provided a powerful political representation of a new phase of capitalist restructuring, combining a reactionary sense of tradition – its Victorian values – with a commitment to modernisation, to move with the times.

Even when faced with vehement opposition it has pursued its project – implementing the poll tax, reforming the welfare state and the NHS, privatising the water authorities – without public support. Its continued tenure of government rests on minority electoral support and a divided and confused opposition.

It is always on the move, attempting to make and remake the political agenda, constantly testing the limits of what is possible in its search to renew the power and wealth of capital. Unafraid to use coercive and authoritarian methods, it is a novel, innovative, hegemonic political force which has moved on from the destruction of the postwar settlement to chart a reactionary course into the new times.

Regressive Radicalism

Thatcherism has changed what is politically possible, in a sweeping conservative transformation which for most people was unthinkable ten years ago. It has coalesced a range of interests behind its programme, not just by offering economic rewards, but also by articulating a range of strongly felt, and popular fears, prejudices and aspirations. It tries always to work with the grain of society, to move it in a rightward direction, implanting its values through practical solutions to social problems. It is driven politically by four linked themes: individualism and authoritarianism, marketisation and privatisation.

Thatcherism has responded to demands for greater autonomy and choice with an ideology of assertive individualism. This offers the alluring myth that individuals can be self-sufficient and do not have to take wider collective responsibility for social problems. So if collective solutions, like state education or the NHS, do not meet individuals' choices, they are encouraged to buy their way out.

This view of individualism is dynamic, because it encourages people to remake their individual worlds. But it is an aggressively conservative view of how society should be organised. It sanctions the marketisation of society and human relations. It upholds the private sector and the market as symbols for flexibility, efficiency and choice. It enfeebles the public sector and represents it as inflexible, inefficient and lacking in choice.

Individual choice appears as a neutral ideology that everyone can ascribe to. But it has justified growing inequality, the collapse of social cohesion and the abandonment of social responsibility. It is Thatcherism's most fundamental and extensive privatisation: the privatisation of social aspiration, obligation and responsibility. There is no such thing as society.

It explains the fundamental nature of Thatcherism's attack on socialism. For it undermines the sense of the social upon which socialism is based, the ideology of equal access to subsistence income for all, to health, education and mobility, which underpins the universalist principles of socialism.

Thatcherism's individualism moves in tandem with an authoritarianism aimed at instilling social and economic discipline. Its authoritarian and repressive agendas on crime, law and order, immigration and sexuality, are a response to the so-called permissiveness of the 1960s, which it blames for causing a collapse of respect for traditional British values.

While its ideology is anti-state, it has both centralised state power and used it more strategically than any previous government. The old public industries which threatened to cloud the dawn of the enterprise economy – coal, shipbuilding, steel, cars – have been restructured. Local government and local education authorities are being stripped of their powers. Police powers have been strengthened; civil liberties, freedom of speech and protest have been undermined. The welfare state has become an increasingly coercive part of its social and economic strategy, to control public spending and to discipline young people and the unemployed into passive acceptance of a Thatcherite work ethic. Trade-union rights have been curtailed by legislation and their voices ignored or ruthlessly repressed.

Its agenda of regressive moral conservativism around sexuality exalts the values of the nuclear family. Lone mothers, the fastest-growing group dependent upon welfare, are presented as irresponsible and undeserving, because they do not fit the traditional, outdated model of the patriarchal nuclear family. Indeed, the family is the only institution which Thatcherism contemplates between the individual and the state.

Thatcherism has also encouraged the rise of corporate authoritarianism. International capital is being given largely free rein to restructure the economy. Privatisation has transferred key sectors from limited public control. Small companies are virtually free to hire and fire at will.

Thatcherism's economic agenda has responded to a deeply-felt pessimism about the weakness of the British economy. Yet it has also elevated the market to a principle of economic organisation, at great social cost: to the 1.7m who lost their jobs in the early 1980s, in terms of long-term investment in training, research and development, and for those without the resources to prosper in the market economy.

All this is draped in the Union Jack. A reactionary Britishness is essential to these ideas of moral order and discipline, respect for the authority of parents, the state, and law and order. And the values of 'enterprise' are the values which 'made Britain great' in the 19th century. This regressive conception of Britishness is also clear in Thatcherism's staunch anti-devolutionism and tacit endorsement of racism.

Thatcherism's approach to international politics veers between strident nationalism and paralysis in the face of US policy and international developments. Yet more than any other politician Thatcher has rammed home the message that Britain's economy cannot be separated from the international economy and international capital.

Class Politics

Class remains central to British politics. There is an enormous gulf between the increasingly concentrated, wealthy and international- ised ruling class which exerts strategic control over financial and industrial capital, and the majority of working people who have to sell their labour to live.

But as society moves into the new times of the 1990s the character of both the ruling class and the working class is changing. Thatcherism has coalesced a range of social support for its politics from these changes. It has fed the wealthy and powerful by placing more of the burden of taxation and the costs of economic change on the poor, the unemployed, and the low-paid. It has delivered control of key parts of the economy into private hands. But it has not simply acted for the ruling class. It has restructured, renovated and internationalised the ruling class itself.

Its early monetarism drove thousands of manufacturing companies out of business. Its relations with the Confederation of British Industry, the main employers' organisation, have been marked by tension. It has consistently favoured upwardly-mobile industrial entrepreneurs as dynamic forces to reinvigorate British capitalism.

Thatcherism has also helped transform British finance capital. Banks and building societies have been opened up to competition. With the 1987 Big Bang in the City of London, foreign banks swallowed up traditional British stockbrokers. The rowdy stock exchange floor, for decades the public face of capitalism's inner sanctum, lies empty, replaced by multinational computer trading.

Thatcherism has dominated and politicised the civil service. It has attacked pillars of the old postwar establishment: the BBC, the universities, the church, and the medical and legal professions. It has transformed the Tory Party, exiling the one-nation Tories responsible for the postwar settlement, re-uniting the rank and file with their autocratic leadership for the first time in decades, by coupling the ideologies of market and moralism.

It does not rely upon any single class or group. It has won substantial backing from the professional, private sector middle classes and the skilled working class, with subsidised private pensions, home ownership, council house sales, share sales, expanded private credit and rising real incomes for those in work. It aims particularly to appeal to the core workers the new economy is creating.

It is widening division within society. The millions

permanently excluded from the affluence it trumpets, are ideologically ostracised as 'scroungers' or 'whingers'. Thatcherism is working with the new times to exacerbate the divisions between employed and unemployed, the skilled, new technology workers and low-paid part-timers.

It has sought to appeal to new social movements and aspirations. For example, its economic policies and moral stance have considerable appeal to conservative Asians. While promoting Christian orthodoxy in the provisions of the new Education Reform Act, it encourages religious fundamentalism. Most recently it has attempted to appeal to people who support the green movement.

Sometimes Thatcherism has made these appeals unconvincingly. For they expose contradictions and tensions within its politics. But its project is to become a hegemonic political force. It should not be assumed that there are automatic limits to how far it can widen that support, even when such limits might seem to have been reached.

Thatcherism and the State

thatcherism's transformation of the state and its relationship with society has been central to its domination of the political agenda of the 1980s.

At parliamentary level, the government has ruthlessly exploited its majority, despite commanding only just over 40 per cent support among voters. It has further centralised prime ministerial power, consistently clashed with the Lords and ignored select committees.

Central control over local government has been dramatically increased through a range of legislation, from poll tax to the abolition of the GLC and metropolitan authorities.

Thatcherism is also privatising intermediary bodies. Thus the tripartite Manpower Services Commission has been replaced by a central Training Agency which will be an offshoot of the Department of Employment. Millions of pounds of spending on training will be controlled by local, private sector-led Training and Enterprise Councils. Private Housing Action Trusts are to replace local authority management of estates.

But the tentacles of Thatcherite influence have reached

further. Institutions in civil society have been harnessed to the government's ideological purpose, thereby transforming their role. So, for instance, the media's ability to assess and report on government activities has been further limited by the new Official Secrets Act and by concerted political attack on the BBC and ITV.

Even those institutions which have long acted as bulwarks of the establishment, such as the churches, have suffered open attack by the government, because they have raised voices in opposition to government policies. The criticism from leading Church of England figures has been met with abrasive counter-attack, personal vetting of senior appointments and attempts to undermine the Church's authority.

By exploiting real concerns over how trade unions represented their members, the Thatcher governments have constrained them within ever narrower limits. The banning of trade unions at GCHQ represented a new attack on the political freedom of state employees, further entrenching the state as a partisan, pro-government institution.

Underpinnning the expansion in state control has been an increased use of coercive powers to stifle democratic opposition. Police powers have grown apace, with increased autonomy, a more political role, more resources and a wider range of offensive equipment. This process started in the 1970s, drawing from Britain's counter-insurgency role in Northern Ireland, but found its fullest expression with the black community's uprisings in the inner cities and during the 1984-85 miners' strike. The active implementation of the Prevention of Terrorism Act and the further suspension of civil liberties in Northern Ireland has followed a period of sustained conflict with the Provisional IRA.

The Thatcher governments have been effective and radical managers of the state. The prime minister and her advisers play a key role in the appointment of senior civil servants to ensure they will effectively deliver the government's programmes. The British state has never been a passive, politically neutral instrument of government. But although Thatcherism still faces opposition from within, it has dominated the state, and now leads it.

the **opposition** *to* *thatcherism*

The most urgent task for progressive politics is to defeat Thatcherism and open the way for a new phase of social reform and progress. But, as we said before, Thatcherism will only be defeated electorally if it is also defeated politically and ideologically.

The hesitant and unevenly developing nature of the opposition to Thatcherism is evident in all the four main areas which have provoked opposition: the costs of Thatcherism's reactionary economic restructuring, the inequality it has created, Thatcherism's authoritarianism and its narrow nationalism.

Economic Restructuring and Trade Unions

throughout the 1980s, unions have been vital in defending workers from more assertive employers, enjoying their enhanced power under the government's trade-union reforms. Industrial struggles have been the focus for much wider political opposition to Thatcherism.

The early opposition to the government's trade-union reforms and the days of action against unemployment were unsuccessful. It was a period of savage capitalist restructuring. It was almost impossible for the labour movement to win major victories in such a hostile climate. Whatever the basic justice of their case, the unions failed to win the moral high ground: their struggles seemed to be a defence of the discredited beer-and-sandwiches machinery of government and an approach to production which many knew to be inefficient. Union opposition to the legislation on pre-strike ballots and general secretary elections did not seem to face up to the widespread view that union leaders were unaccountable and unrepresentative.

The year-long heroic miners' strike of 1984-85 was pivotal in the development of the labour movement's opposition to

Thatcherism. It was met with the most ruthless mobilisation of the state machine against the miners and their families. It contained many lessons for future struggles.

The union concentration on picketing as a major tactic and the refusal to have a national ballot limited its public support. Yet the strikers' determined fight took them far beyond the issues of a simple wage dispute. This, and the strikers' reliance on the total involvement of entire communities, created opportunities for a new politics. Broad support was won among trade unions, churches, gays, lesbians and black communities. Outstanding was the role of the women's groups, which saw the need to appeal to all sections of the community. Women were being empowered to challenge entrenched sexism and to participate creatively and autonomously in political activity to which they brought their own distinctive aims and ideas. Unfortunately these new avenues were not later developed.

As the union movement enters the 1990s it is increasingly debating how to modernise, rather than whether to modernise. Unions have had some success in turning aspects of the Tories' anti-union legislation to their advantage, such as with ballots for political funds and taking industrial action.

Most are coming to terms with changes in the labour market: through mergers, by offering new services to members and by developing new recruitment and bargaining strategies.

The health workers' campaign to defend the NHS is in some ways a model of modernisation. It has fostered wide popular support, because the health workers have been acting for society as well as for themselves. The unprecedented public battle has been waged by such a broad range of forces as the BMA, hospital doctors and GPs, nurses and heath workers, local authorities and patients, as well as most political parties and public bodies. This breadth offers an outstanding opportunity for the unions and the labour movement to help create a vast, united social movement around a modern defence of a national health service.

The unions are also becoming alert to the opportunities and dangers of European integration. Europeanisation could offer unions an important new role in the 1990s, representing the interests of all workers, whether unionised or not, in Brussels.

As the unions have started to modernise, so they have

become better able to voice the concerns of their members and people more generally. As a result they could become more effective opponents of Thatcherism in the workplace and society at large.

Economic Ideology

thatcherism's command of the economic agenda has been vital to its success. It started with an appeal for collective belt-tightening to rid Britain of inflation and inefficiency. This popular but authoritarian monetarist ideology was central to the election of the first Thatcher government in 1979. In the mid-1980s, it shifted to promoting selective prosperity. This was vital to its re-election in 1987.

But Thatcherism now seems to have lost its command of the economic agenda. There is a persistent worry that its economic recovery was both stunted and ill-founded. The economy has become dangerously depal services and interest on overseas loans. Tax cuts and increasing use of credit have financed a retail boom – a fragile prosperity which has sucked in imports and produced a huge balance of payments deficit.

The extension of home ownership and personal credit have left increasing numbers of people extremely vulnerable to high interest rates. Retirement, childbirth, or redundancy can quickly push people from the building society to the debt collector. The consequences of industrial deregulation and new economic pressures have been dramatically seen in the tragedies of Zeebrugge, Kings Cross, Clapham and other disasters. These tragedies have shown how workers, consumers and environmentalists might come together in new alliances to challenge government's priority of profit over people's lives.

At the beginning of the 1980s the challenge to Thatcherism's economic ideology was led by the traditional doctrines of Keynesian demand management and reflation, articulated by professors in universities. At the end of the decade the challenge is being led, much more successfully, by the green movement in society, which popularises scientific concerns for the future of the planet and voices a demand for responsible and sustainable development. It seems likely that the industrialised world will be faced in the 1990s with hard choices and a need to revise the current growth imperative.

The government is more vulnerable on the economy than for many years. But an alternative, modernising economic programme – which takes responsibility for managing interest rates and renewing our industrial infrastructure – will be vital to winning support for the opposition. It will need to be sophisticated enough to cope with the diverse and sometimes antagonistic interests of producers and consumers, or conflicting pressures for growth and ecological renewal. And its popularisation will be crucial for it to become the property of millions.

Inequality

Opposition to Thatcherism's deepening of social inequality and division has been persistent. But the form and approach it has taken has altered during the 1980s.

Thatcherism's restructuring is widening the chasm between the increasing numbers of people forced into ever deeper poverty, and the other two thirds of society enjoying relative – though highly differentiated – affluence. The number of households officially accepted as homeless has doubled since 1979. About 4m disabled people were judged to be 'just getting by', according to a recent official survey. More than 5.5m pensioners are surviving on low incomes.

The early 1980s were dominated by struggles against 'the Cuts'. 'The Cuts' were real, sharp and painful. But they were also metaphors for all that was wrong with Thatcherism's attack on the public sector, and the society it stood for.

With the destruction of great swathes of the productive sector, notably mining, shipbuilding and the indigenous car industry, the key metaphor for inequality in the late 1980s has become the 'north-south' divide. It is a metaphor for something wrong in society, rather than simply the institutions of the welfare state.

Thatcherism's policies have also energised institutions and constituencies which were politically subdued in the 1970s. It was the combination of 'exclusion' from society and heavy policing which produced the urban riots of the early 1980s. The church has led the way in condemning Thatcherism's celebration of inequality and competition. Its moral challenge has also become a focus for alternative policies, for instance through the Archbishop of Canterbury's *Faith in the City* inquiry into the inner city.

Concern over inequality ensures continued support for state-provided welfare, for the NHS and child benefit, and in the opposition to the poll tax and further tax cuts for the well-off.

So there is a widespread desire for a more cohesive, compassionate society. But as yet this has mainly been a defensive movement. It has yet to develop into a forward-looking movement around a new agenda for health and welfare for the 1990s.

Authoritarianism

thatcherism's traditional Victorian values breed a social authoritarianism which has further politicised sexuality, family relations and everyday life. It has stoked prejudice against gays and lesbians. But Clause 28 was defiantly contested by an impressively broad alliance of opposition forces.

The authority of the respectable nuclear family is at the core of Thatcherism's attempt to reassert social discipline. Yet its family ideal is increasingly at odds with the reality of many people's lives. Deep-rooted concern about child abuse was first brought out by the television programme *Childwatch* and subsequently in the Cleveland affair. There is also increasing awareness of the problem of male violence within the family.

Thus, as the 1980s have progressed, the central role of the family is coming under increasing strain. As a consequence Thatcherism's support among women has declined. Contrary to popular myth that women voted for Thatcher because she was a woman, all three general elections in which she triumphed have been characterised by a haemorrhaging of support among women and a rightward shift among men.

But it is the authoritarianism of Thatcher's state which has provoked most open conflict.

In the early to mid-1980s, Thatcherism's assault on local government provoked anti-rate capping campaigns and policies of defiance, which reached their peak in Liverpool in 1986. But many people saw these as sectarian left campaigns to defend councils which had long offered many people poor services. During the decade, that opposition has broadened and become more sophisticated.

In the early 1980s few Labour local authorities had economic development policies which went beyond offering rate subsidies. But in the late 1980s Labour councils in towns such as Swindon, Southampton, Norwich, Birmingham and Sheffield are developing approaches which involve working in alliance with the private sector, voluntary associations and enterprise agencies to promote more socially responsible forms of economic development.

Scotland: a Case Study of Resistance

Scotland provides the most striking example of how the opposition to Thatcherism has developed over the decade. Since the 1979 election, when the majority voted for parties other than the Tories, Scotland has been governed without consent.

Thatcher's use of Scotland as a guinea pig for the poll tax, its attempt to anglicise Scottish education and law, its aim of breaking the established pattern of publicly owned housing and its increased centralisation, have helped create a new sense of national awareness and energy for self-determination in the late 1980s.

It is no longer only about 1970s-style devolution. The opinion poll support for independence now runs at around 35 per cent and between 18-25 year-olds, closer to 50 per cent. This new mood has found expression in the Scottish Constitutional Convention – representing 80 per cent of the Scottish people through their institutions and organisations – which is united in the fight for a Scottish Assembly or parliament.

The change of mood is also reflected in the rise in support for the SNP and in a resurgence of Scottish popular culture, through events such as Mayfest, and many writers, poets, painters, journalists, and rock bands.

There is a new confidence in Scotland's aspiration for self-determination which is emerging along with the possibility that small nations can find a new role in a more integrated Europe.

But most importantly the movement for self-determination has come from the Scottish TUC and the work of the Scottish trade unions, which have been committed to working in alliance with other movements in society. This has created the basis for new relationships between political parties, including the Labour Party, the Democrats, the Communist Party, the SNP, and a broad movement in society, including the churches. The Communist Party has made an important contribution to developing unity, although many problems remain in overcoming narrow 'party political' approaches.

Key to the rise of the STUC has been its involvement on a wide range of issues over the last three decades: from the struggle to locate industry in Scotland and the fight against Polaris in the 1960s, to the present-day campaign for a Scottish parliament.

The movement for Scottish self-determination stands a chance of success because it combines the elements required to defeat Thatcherism. It is based around a forward-looking and active labour movement; it is promoting new alliances between the political parties and the Scottish people in the Constitutional Convention. It has a clear ideological appeal focused on democracy and self-determination. Its popularity spreads not just through politics, but popular culture as well.

Nationalism and Internationalism

Thatcherism's 'British values' have a specific, reactionary, English, south-eastern inflection. This attachment to a narrow nationalism has always gone hand in hand with an openness to international capital seeking to acquire British business and general support for US foreign policy.

The contradictions of this open and closed approach to Britain's role in the world contain one of Thatcherism's deepest vulnerabilities. For instance, the Westland crisis, which led to the resignation of Michael Heseltine and the sacking of Leon Brittan, was essentially about whether Britain's industrial future lay with Europe or America.

Jacques Delors, President of the European Commission, has recently come to be seen as one of Mrs Thatcher's chief opponents. In the next few years European opposition to Thatcherism will become more important as Britain's future becomes inextricably tied to that of Europe as a whole.

The mass peace movement of the early 1980s was vital in creating the conditions for the popular international disarmament initiatives of perestroika. It also paved the way for the internationalist movements of the late 1980s. The Falklands War stoked up regressive, militaristic, nationalistic feeling in 1982. But Live Aid, Sport Aid, Comic Relief, the Mandela concert and the response to the Armenian earthquake both revealed and promoted a popular mood of progressive, humanitarian internationalism in the late 1980s.

Ideology and Parties

The opposition to Thatcherism has partially modernised. But one fact is overriding. Thatcherism is far from defeated. It is still an immensely powerful, innovating, mobile political force. It is far from exhausted. It has tremendous resources to destabilise, marginalise, crush or absorb opposition.

The various currents of opposition need to be brought into a coherent but flexible political and ideological framework. Progressive social movements in the 1980s have been fundamentally weakened by the opposition parties' failure to challenge Thatcherism politically. But the common purpose of the opposition cannot simply be the defeat of Thatcherism. It must be a vision of how the popular defeat of Thatcherism – involving millions of people – could usher in a new phase of popular social progress.

In part that vision will emerge from the common strands which give the opposition to Thatcherism its energy. It will be a vision of a more compassionate, socially cohesive society, less authoritarian, more democratic. It will be a society committed to conservation and ecological renewal, the promotion of international co-operation and development, and a sustainable economic modernisation.

It is up to the opposition parties, and particularly the Labour Party, to synthesise, energise and give voice to the anti-Thatcher majority in society. As yet they have failed in that task. Thatcherism has never won more than 42 per cent of the vote. Yet it has not been threatened electorally. Despite repeated attempts at renewal Labour still appears incapable of illuminating a vision of social progress which matches the needs and aspirations of the new times.

Labour's crisis is not a set of election defeats, but its failure to modernise. It has grown estranged from the society it seeks to govern, unable either to come to terms with the dissolution, contraction and transformation of its old working-class constituencies, or to reach out to rising social forces. It retains a conservative commitment to the supremacy of parliamentary politics, to the central state and the British union. The Labour Party has signally failed to campaign successfully on the issues that affect people's lives.

For all its problems and weaknesses, Labour remains the predominant channel for progressive centre-left opinion in electoral terms. Indeed, Labour's traditional association with organised workers gives it an electoral stability that the centre parties lack. But with the formation of the SLD and the SDP, and the increased support for the Green Party, British politics are never again likely to be dominated by just two parties.

But signs of renewal are now appearing, with the Labour Party's policy reviews, its moves to extend inner-party democracy, and the SLD's document, *Our Different Vision*. The issue of electoral pacts and agreements – and thus how to reverse the fragmentation of the early 1980s – is on the political agenda.

For the immediate future the need to defeat Thatcher is such that electoral agreement should be sought between the opposition parties at the next election. If this can't be reached nationally on an agreed programme of government, then it should be sought in marginal constituencies on a more limited basis.

a **vision** *for the 1990s*

We need a vision of a new society for the new times. It must have the stature to match the significance of the changes underway in society. It must stand for a new stage of progressive social development.

The great themes of progressive politics in the 1990s will emerge in response to the changes underway in British society. While it is inconceivable that all the diverse strands can or should be encompassed within a single and fixed ideological framework, any credible political force has to have a strategy for how society would resolve the key issues, and thereby develop over the next decade.

There are nine central issues society must address:

World peace and disarmament: Peace is more than just the absence of war, it is a positive condition in which states solve differences by civilised, legal means. The aim must be to reach a level of armaments which is demonstrably defensive and threatens no other state. More immediately, the international community must take responsibility for bringing to an end the various regional conflicts around the world.

Ecological crisis: There is a surge of popular desire underway for more sustainable forms of production and consumption. The green movement, from Friends of the Earth and Greenpeace to the National Trust, is speaking and campaigning for millions. It is underpinned by a powerful ideology: a new public ethic of shared responsibility for the future of the planet. The goal of this movement should be to establish a progressive environmental settlement between society and nature, which would allow both to develop through peaceful interdependence.

Internationalisation of production and politics: The globalising of capitalism, the reshaping of Europe, perestroika's foreign policy and the crisis of world development, are creating irresistible pressures towards a new internationalism. Britain should aim in the 1990s to promote a new international humanism. This would focus foreign policy on contributing to the process of disarmament, European co-operation to end the divide between East and West and the creation of new international institutions to promote inter-dependence and sustainable development.

The crisis of social cohesion, care and compassion: A new popular ethic of social citizenship, equal life chances and of society as our common home is emerging. A political commitment to social cohesion in the 1990s would have a universal appeal, but would, importantly, redistribute in favour of the poor.

The crisis of male society: The rise in women's paid employ-ment, changing patterns of marriage, separation and divorce, are creating pressures for extensive legal and social reform. Unions should place women at the centre of their collective bargaining agenda.

Eroding male privilege will be vital to the democratisation of power exercised daily in the high street, the workplace and the home. Similarly, the powerful assertion of heterosexuality as the norm must be undermined if the widespread inequality experienced by lesbians and gay men is to be ended.

A central goal of the next decade must be a progressive settlement between women, men and the institutions which mediate human relations.

The future of work: Mass unemployment, the new working practices demanded by new technology, the changing nature of the labour force and work patterns, all mean society should reassess the organisation and distribution of employment.

The labour movement's strategic aim for the next decade should be to match a commitment to productive, enterprising work, with social obligations to full employment, the redistribution of work and improved conditions of employment.

The modernisation of the economy: The first goal of the 1990s must be to overcome the ravages inflicted by the laissez-faire policies of the last decade and the historic decline of manufacturing industry. But the longer-term aim must be to establish a new economic settlement between the demands of modernisation and the needs of the environment.

The future of British democracy: A new democratic ethic is emerging from numerous campaigns, most notably Charter 88, calling for a new democratic settlement between the powers of the state and the rights of the citizen, through the decentralisation of power, accountability of public institutions and bodies, new citizenship rights and the extension of civil liberties.

The future of Britain's nations: The same agenda of nationhood which is now predominant throughout the world, also goes to the heart of Britain's constitutional crisis. So within any new democratic settlement there must be some form of federalism which enhances national rights and regional devolution, within a refashioned Europe.

The search for a solution to the conflict in Northern Ireland requires that the isolation of the Irish crisis from British politics must end. Alongside the campaign for the overall disengagement of British control over part of Ireland, there must be wide-ranging democratic reforms in Northern Ireland.

A new deal for the new times: There are already significant indications of a burgeoning democratic and humanitarian alternative to Thatcherite ideology. This needs to be nurtured so that a new popular common sense can infuse the wide variety of social movements which will provide the motive force for progressive advance in the next decade.

The great reforms after the war were designed to lift social relations, human needs, desires and aspirations beyond the vagaries of the free market. The wave of social reform we have in mind is in line with the *principles* of that tradition.

The postwar reforms were bound by a central link – that individual aspirations were most effectively satisfied by collective solutions. The new progressive politics develops new links between individual aspirations and collective solutions to social problems. Ecological and internationalist politics link individuals with a global collective. A new international politics would also link in to an emerging European identity. Civil liberties and individual rights are inextricably bound up with a society and a state which would be more democratic for everyone.

Like the social reforms after the war, these settlements would redistribute resources in favour of the least powerful and the worst-off. But they would learn from the failures of the postwar settlement. They would redistribute power: empowering women rather than men, the local against the central, the individual against the state and the corporation, workers rather than capital, communities blighted by pollution rather than the corporations which produce it.

The progressive politics would reunite us with the humanitarian traditions of the early socialists who were concerned with the politics of consumption, art, culture, poetry, nature, childhood and sexuality, as well as production. Socialism would be recovered as a bottom-up, dynamic, humanising force by these developments.

After ten ·cold years of Thatcherism a new stage of social progress is now within sight. But the common vision we have outlined needs to be given shape and colour by the parties, movements, and groups in progressive politics.

a **different** *kind of politics*

The new times are transforming the character of politics – how it is conducted, what it is about, where it takes place. But politics is also shaping the new times. Thatcherism, Gorbachev, the green movement – all these are agenda-setting, shaping society's responses to new issues. The crisis of the Left in Britain is its failure to find a political role appropriate to the epochal shift occurring in the organisation of society.

This failure is intimately connected to the Left's inability to reorient itself in recognition of Britain's changing social composition.

Reconstructing the Social

two dimensions of change stand out. Firstly, the combined impact of new technology and neo-liberal economic policies, coming in the wake of longer-term social change, has finally fractured the traditional class identities and cultures which provided the Left's foundations. And secondly, the last 30 years have seen the emergence of social movements focusing on issues outside the workplace. The rise of these popular movements, deploying novel forms of involvement and campaigning, is an historic change in the range and character of political forces.

Between 1926 and 1988, the proportion of people in the UK employed in service industries rose from 33 per cent to 69 per cent, a mirror image of the relative decline in those employed in manufacturing and production: from 68 per cent to 31 per cent.

In recent years these long-term trends have sharpened. At the same time, women are on the way to becoming half the workforce, heavily concentrated in 'caring' roles in service industries, frequently in a part-time capacity.

The rise and persistence of mass, long-term unemployment means there is a crucial division between those in and those out of work. Many in the working class now possess assets beyond their labour power in the form of savings, inheritance, and property. These resources cushion them against insecurity in marked contrast with the position of the long-term unemployed and the underclass in the inner cities.

None of these changes mean that Britain is becoming less of a class society. It has become a more unequal, more exploitative society. But the traditions of class do not provide such a strong point of common identity, commitment and purpose. Your chances of power, income and wealth are as likely to be determined by whether you are a man or a woman, black or white.

We all now wear different identities which we take up and discard with amazing rapidity and ease: teachers in one capacity, we are parents in another; producers in one situation, we are consumers in the next; members of a family, part of a workforce; hillwalkers today, motorised polluters of the countryside tomorrow and so on.

So, central to the modernisation of class politics will be a strategy which recognises the diverse experiences of class and can match this with a sense of community.

Vital to that sense will be an understanding of the distinctive character of women's oppression. Women will be the core of the working class in the 1990s. But their jobs are still disproportionately lower paid, less skilled, and less secure than men's.

But the obstacles which prevent women determining the shape of their lives stem from a system of oppression by men as well as exploitation by employers. For most women have not only to undertake their paid employment, but also to provide the bulk of unpaid domestic household services for men and children and to bear the brunt of providing care for elderly people.

Social norms, values and male violence – embedded in education, advertising, television and the popular culture of heterosexuality – consign women to subordinate roles. Women's demands over employment, childcare, education, welfare, male violence, law and order and cultural sexism will have to be integral to a successful modernisation of class and progressive politics in the 1990s.

Similar recognition must be given to black people, who are twice as likely as whites to be unemployed and who are disproportionately represented in the peripheral labour force of the new times as contract cleaners, late-night security guards, petrol pump attendants and fast-food workers. Racial inequalities cannot be reduced to class. There is a systematic racist oppression which runs through the state and social institutions, including those of the working class.

Low pay, racist housing allocations and poverty means black people make up 60 per cent of London's homeless. Their entitlement to health and welfare benefits is conditional on passing increasingly stringent, arbitrary immigration controls, which set an official seal on racism in society. They are ten times more likely to be stopped and searched by the police than whites, even though they are also the subject of 7,000 racial attacks a year.

Women and black people have developed distinctive and autonomous forms of struggle. Nor are they alone: the last 30 years have seen a proliferation of political struggles ranging from community politics, through environmental and aid organisations, to the mass peace movement.

The impact of these popular movements reflects their success in appealing to people's diverse interests and aspirations. They illustrate tellingly the potential of autonomous movements for tapping into our different identities.

The Failure of the Political Left

Such profound shifts inevitably create pressure for corresponding changes in the organisation of politics and parties. As yet the labour movement has been unable and unwilling to risk the scale of change required of it.

The main point of a political realignment in the 1990s would be to establish a new conversation between the Left and society. In particular, the labour movement has become out of touch with people's real concerns and is in danger of ending up in a corner talking to itself.

There are six fundamental ways in which our whole conception of politics is being challenged. In all six, Thatcherism has responded to change much more effectively than the labour movement.

Firstly, there is the expansion of the realm of politics over the last 30 years. Our personal lives, from consumption to sexuality, have become increasingly politicised. Politics is less and less confined to a distinct realm of parties, resolutions, manifestos and elections. The agents of political change have become more diverse and complex.

One of Thatcherism's great strengths has been its drive to embed its politics in civil society, through cultural change: the enterprise culture, the spread of Thatcherite personal identities of home-owner, credit-card holder and share-owner; and through instilling new social ethics of value for money, choice, efficiency.

Secondly, the expansion of politics in society has contributed to changing the role of the state. The idea of the state managing society, playing an extensive role in delivering solutions and services, is being superseded.

There is a widespread desire for a state which is capable of taking determined, strategic action to sort out problems. But this is matched by a desire for a less intrusive, paternalistic state, allowing people to reach their own solutions to problems.

Thatcherism has understood the need to transform the state. It has used it much more strategically and ruthlessly than any previous government. And it also has a clear idea of a right-wing enabling state. Much of its legislation, on privatisation, council house sales and trade-union reform, has been aimed at enabling its supporters.

By contrast, the labour movement has a conservative approach to the state. It wants to occupy the state, when the state needs to be transformed. It supports the current electoral system, it accepts the British union and is conservative on issues like a bill of rights. It is deeply defensive of its main historic achievement – the corporatist, Keynesian welfare state. It needs instead to be a radical reformer.

Thirdly, politics and power are becoming increasingly internationalised. Thatcherism is riven with an insular chauvinism which means it will never be able to adjust fully to internationalisation. But the labour movement has responded even more inadequately. Its political arena is almost exclusively that of the nation state.

Fourthly, the depth and force of new times changes require radical new thinking. To steer society through uncharted territory, politics has to have wide horizons, clear values which command popular support and the confidence to innovate.

Thatcherism has excelled at providing values and innovative policies, arising out of the intellectual renewal of the Right from the mid-1970s on, which was based around a web of right-wing think tanks. Thatcherism has had the confidence to take risks. The Left has yet to match its confidence.

Fifthly, social upheaval has been accompanied by the fragmentation of old political constituencies and social allegiances. This has been accompanied by the rise of new sources of collective identity and attachment, which do not readily fit the old political straitjackets of Right or Left. While the labour movement has been unable to come to terms with the decline of its old constituencies among the male, mainly white manufacturing class, Thatcherism has much more effectively realigned itself with rising social groups and aspirations – the affluent working class, entrepreneurial businessmen, and the meritocratic private sector middle class.

Sixthly, the transition to new times is creating a sharp new political cleavage: between those who have shifted on to the terrain of the new era and those who still hanker after the familiar past. Thus, alongside 'left' and 'right' we need a new vocabulary to describe political polarities.

Socialism has always claimed to speak for the future. But in the last fifteen years its authority to do so has been thrown into doubt by these six developments, prompting some fundamental questions about the links between socialism and progress.

One of the most inspiring examples of how to respond to these questions creatively has been provided by Gorbachev. Perestroika is creative because it takes risks with the meaning of socialism. The role of the party, planning and the state are being redefined. Gorbachev talks of a new socialist morality of enterprise, individual responsibility and initiative within Soviet society. He has confidently rejected the old polarities of the cold war. Instead he talks about common human values, self-determination and pluralism.

The malaise of the Left is that the old is dying but the new is still struggling to be born. We are searching for a new political language. Embarking on this search is risky. But it is inescapable: social change and political failure is driving us in that direction.

Paths to Renewal

The Left will only be renewed if it can encompass society's change in a modern, progressive, political form. And that means, crucially, a new set of relationships between social movements, unions and political parties, in mobilising people, expressing aspirations, challenging power and enacting change.

The rise of social movements, such as feminism and the green movement, has partially dislodged the political party as a unifier of political demands. But the social movements have been weakened by the failure of the opposition parties. Parties remain critical for two reasons: firstly, they form governments which can exercise an important measure of control over the state and enable change in civil society. Secondly, they act as a vital focal point for social coalitions.

The social movements are extremely diverse in form, objective and duration: some are more issue-based, while others are essentially about social and personal identity. But they share some important central characteristics.

They challenge capitalism's separation of production from its consequences and from the sphere of reproduction (by which we mean the reproduction of daily life, of the conditions of production itself and of the environment).

They deploy flexible forms of organisation which allow people greater choice about how to become involved in politics. They do not constrain politics to a single area or a single sense of identity. Most combine a social philosophy with a personal political practice.

As well as being visionary, they are all deeply practical. All involve people in direct challenges to power, yet they are realistic about the process of political change. Feminism, for instance, has revealed the social power which oppresses women – from paid employment through to the culture of advertising and the social norms of familial, heterosexual life – to be much more diverse and complex than much of the socialist Left had appreciated. Feminism's idea of emancipation is both more complete, more practical and more gradual than many of the established ideas of social transformation embedded in the traditional Left.

The social movements are a response to new aspirations

and problems. They are in touch with society because they live and breathe within society, rather than pacing the musty corridors of narrow institutional power. However, the links between sets of ideas, social movements and what is popular is not straightforward. And the relationships between different social movements with different aims can be troublesome and conflictual. How most effectively to construct broad, popular alliances which do not stifle these movements is an unresolved question.

The unions stand between the social movements and the Labour Party. They have one foot in the issues which confront people in their everyday lives and the other in formal politics. A daily confrontation with restructuring at work, and the changing make-up of the workforce, as well as the shifting aspirations and needs of their own memberships, are forcing the unions to modernise. Industrial restructuring is shifting the main centres of unionisation to the public service sector and producing new key constituencies of union membership, such as women. Yet unlike the social movements, the unions have very formal, hierarchical structures which link them to the Labour Party. At the heart of the unions' modernisation must be a new combination of their industrial, social and political roles.

The unions have a long tradition of activity and campaigning for broad progressive measures as part of a wider social vision. During much of the postwar period the unions stood not just for their members, but for progress through expanding employment and welfare. In the 1970s, however, they became increasingly successfully portrayed by the Right as unrepresentative, sectional interests, acting for their members against the interests of wider society.

The unions need to become a bridge between the social movements, the voluntary sector, pressure groups and the Labour Party. In taking up women's demands over childcare provision, discrimination and flexible working time, the demands of black and ethnic minority workers for full citizenship, in work and in the community, the demands of the green movement over sustainable production, and the interests of all workers in the rights that might come with Europeanisation, the unions should establish their wider role: helping to create and transmit values of social solidarity. They would also give these political expression through the Labour

Party, because the future of the unions' political role does not lie in breaking their links with Labour, but rather in recasting them.

But the unions also need to modernise their broader political role. For instance, in electricity and water privatisation unions should articulate consumers' concerns about quality of services, price rises and the protection of the countryside. They should be developing a political strategy on issues such as the poll tax and 35-hour week.

Finally, the traditional role of political parties is being disrupted by the extension of politics into civil society and the new forms of expression being thrown up around the issues of new times. The old, rigid divisions of power and function between the personal and the political, the state and civil society, parliamentary politics and extra-parliamentary activity, no longer apply.

Whether and in what form a new, multi-faceted politics emerges will depend on the character of renewal of the Labour Party. Like a Fordist factory it has long chains of command and a strict division of labour. Discipline, bureaucracy and hierarchy predominate over initiative, flexibility and manoeuvrability. It offers people only a limited role in politics. The branch has specific, limited tasks, within a pyramid of political management. Branch life is not about people as political agents, changing themselves or society around them. It is about winning votes, passing resolutions, internalising rather than projecting politics.

These, then, are the components of realignment: the social movements, the unions and the Labour Party. Realignment should create a broad, progressive politics capable of moving through all spheres of society. The process of realignment will have two linked stages. Firstly, the defeat of Thatcherism, which will be more quickly achieved if Labour reaches some form of political and electoral agreement with the smaller opposition parties. But this must open the way to a more permanent realignment of progressive forces liaised on a very different style of democratic activity and participatory politics.

Defeating Thatcherism

the importance of preventing another Tory victory is so great that it should in the next few years determine the approach of all democratic political parties who want Britain to develop differently.

The central issue here is not whether Labour might under the present electoral system win a majority of seats with the votes of a minority of the electorate. Rather, it is that defeating Thatcherism, reversing its consequences and opening the way to progressive change, requires the active support of a majority of the British people. Such a majority cannot be mobilised at the present time by any one party alone; it requires effective agreement between a range of parties and movements.

There are some forms of political and electoral agreements which will not work. An agreement, for example, to share out parliamentary seats based on the lowest common denominator of rehashed old policies would almost certainly fail. Any electoral agreement needs to have political foundations; to open the way to a political future beyond the defeat of Thatcherism.

Those political foundations must be laid now. A wide range of groups opposed to Thatcherism – the unions, green campaigners, the peace movement, nationalists, the church – need to be drawn into campaigning alliances and debate over a joint programme of government. There is already some measure of agreement on a wide range of policy declarations between Labour, the Democrats, Greens, SDP, Communists and nationalist parties.

An agreement on policies will only emerge from a wider political consensus about the priorities for change, requiring a groundswell of public and mass movement support. It is vital that the opposition parties meet their responsibilities to society by settling differences and agreeing those priorities.

Such an alliance, involving as it must, substantial sacrifices by the participating parties of their own cherished policies, will be of limited scope and duration. It is vital therefore that its manifesto should include an undertaking to introduce, if elected to office, an agreed system of proportional representation for the conduct of future parliamentary elections.

The abolition of the present 'elective dictatorship' is an important democratic reform and can, if properly presented, attract widespread popular support. Labour's resistance to democratic electoral reform is an obstacle to it achieving its full voting potential and becoming the accepted leader of an anti-Thatcher alliance.

Renewal

It is impossible to say in detail what the longer-term renewal and realignment of the Left might entail. But the history of other major realignments gives some clues.

It will almost certainly involve not just new ideas, but an intellectual revolution, to map out a new vision of progress, new social values and new ideas about how they should be implemented. Developing these ideas will require political pluralism. The ideas of the Liberals – Keynes and Beveridge – were vital to the labour movement's agenda after the second world war. Their ideas on economic and welfare policy had historic stature. They also produced very practical plans for changing institutions.

Thatcherism's ideological offensive proceeded through a plethora of think tanks and informal groups, creating a new political and intellectual right-wing culture. Much of Thatcherism's class-based agenda is still drawn from businessmen and part-time politicians on the fringes of formal politics.

The Left needs to develop similarly. It has to move from a defensive culture of criticism, towards a creative, risk-taking intellectual culture. Socialists also need to recover past traditions of non-statist, humanist socialism – of the British and international co-operative movements, for instance – which were pushed aside as the labour movement burrowed into the bunkers of the state.

We need another revolution, in political decision-making for the new times to involve a wide diversity of social movements. New forms of democracy, at a local and national level, will be vital.

The internationalisation of politics means that the labour movement has to internationalise itself. This is already happening among unions. The TUC is playing a leading role over the European single market and individual unions are opening up European agendas on collective bargaining, which can be extended beyond workplace issues into wider concerns of European society. International links will be vital to the Left in the 1990s, to co-ordinate common perspectives but also to fertilise ideas.

Finally, it is almost certain that this sort of realignment will require significant changes in the contours of political parties and the relationships between them. The Tory Party itself cannot remain immune from change. Among the opposition, it is possible that an entirely new progressive socialist party for the new times may emerge, incorporating a range of existing parties. More likely, however, realignment will involve some form of federation or strategic alliance between the opposition parties. For the forseeable future, the Tory and Labour Parties are likely to remain the main poles of electoral politics, with a shifting pattern of alliances involving other political forces. The overriding objective must be to obtain agreement on the introduction of proportional representation.

the **communist** *party*

The long struggle for social advance and socialist change in modern times is for communists as much a vision today as it was for the early pioneers, based on the recognition that people have to work collectively to achieve a fair and just society.

The Communist Party shares the past and present of the British Left – its victories and defeats, strengths and weaknesses. It was formed in 1920, in the wake of the first world war and the Russian Revolution, mainly by members of a number of Marxist groups in association with militant trade unionists. Its activity and development have been influenced by several traditions: the Levellers, the Chartists and Utopian Socialists; the labour movement, the unions and co-operative movement; the Leninist tradition and the Third International; and finally the new social movements and their networks in society.

The party's early years were dominated by three streams of thought and action: its relationship with the Labour Party; its affiliation to the Communist International, which directed the activities of Communist Parties being formed throughout the world; and its involvement with working-class communities, especially through the trade unions, culminating in the 1926 general strike.

In its emphasis on work within the union movement, the party has always acknowledged the unions' potential as being much wider than just addressing wages issues: but rather that of giving working people the confidence and power to help move society in a socialist direction.

Relations with the Labour Party were decisively influenced for many years by the rejection of all the party's applications for affiliation and the exclusion of communists from individual Labour Party membership. This was mainly due to the party's membership of and adherence to the Communist International, many of whose decisions in the late 1920s and early 1930s were determined by Stalinist thinking and were wrong and harmful to left unity and the work of the British and other communist parties.

Nevertheless, throughout the 1920s, 30s and 40s the party played an important part in defending the social conditions of millions of workers; in the unemployed workers' movement; the battle for decent housing at fair rents; the development of a mass, militant trade-union movement; in nurturing a socialist tradition in the labour movement; in the development of a Marxist tradition among intellectuals; in the struggle in support of Republican Spain and against Fascism at home and abroad; in solidarity with national liberation movements; and for peace and disarmament.

In the postwar years, but especially since the 20th Congress of the Communist Party of the Soviet Union (CPSU) in 1956, the party has increasingly opposed Stalinist thinking and practices. It has tried, albeit often too slowly, to root decisively its political culture in British society rather than accept a model from another political culture. This development in the life of the party can be seen from 1947 in the ideas developed in the pamphlet *Looking Ahead*, and subsequently in the various editions of the *British Road to Socialism*, which represented an important contribution to the reclamation of an independent British Marxist tradition. The first edition in 1951 rejected an insurrectionary seizure of power as historically outmoded. Later editions outlined a commitment to political pluralism.

Most tellingly though, the party opposed the military interventions in Czechoslovakia in 1968 and Afghanistan in 1979, martial law in Poland, the cultural revolution in China and the treatment of dissent in socialist countries.

The struggle against Stalinism and the process of coming to grips with British realities was protracted. It became clearer in the 1970s when the party began to challenge not only certain traditional axioms of Stalinism but also much of the labour movement's accepted wisdom. Communists developed the concept of the broad democratic alliance: of sharing responsibility for struggles with a plurality of movements and agencies.

In the 1980s, the break with Stalinism led to a rupture in the party. A sectarian grouping succeeded in destroying the party's special relationship with the *Morning Star* and took control of the paper. Subsequently a breakaway organisation was formed.

The Communist Party has emerged from these traumatic years smaller, less well equipped in membership and organisation, but with a commitment to a more democratic identity: to political pluralism. A participative democratic politics is being developed in which minorities can contest attempts to control, fix or suppress opinion. Moreover, traumatic though this period has been, it means the party has taken responsibility for its past – above all the negative aspects of its past – perhaps more than any other tradition on the Left.

Nevertheless, many people, both inside and outside the Communist Party, question whether it any longer plays a valid role in British politics or indeed whether the party has any realistic future.

The need for a strong, independent socialist party in Britain is as important now as it has ever been. The Communist Party today is a party of analysis, strategy and struggle: each function being integrated with the others.

The Communist Party's culture is defined by the importance of thought as well as practice, of ideology as well as struggle, of movements of protest rather than the administration of the state, and by its objective of revolutionary transformation rather than social democracy. It is from this standpoint that the party's involvement is essential in the realignment of the Left in the 1990s. In turn, the party recognises that it must be prepared to change, renew and restructure itself to be able to make its fullest possible contribution to that realignment.

The party's longstanding commitment to the politics of alliance, and its insight into the crisis of the Left, mean that it can act as an important agency, locally and nationally, in facilitating aspects of realignment, as the old divisions and polarities of politics break down.

The Communist Party in recent years has also been one of the central arenas for intellectual renewal on the Left. It has a clear role still as a promoter of ideas and a vehicle for debate and discussion: a 'think-tank' of the Left, not least through its magazine, *Marxism Today*.

The party has performed this function effectively because it has been prepared to learn from others and has never restricted its politics to a narrow party conception. It recognises and values the role of intellectuals, while not separating the thinkers from the doers.

The role of the Communist Party in the mass struggles of the labour and democratic movements is a central reason for the existence of the party as part of the Left. It works, very consciously, for demands that can build a sense of common purpose among people against the worst features of our present society. It is a party of socialism, and has a distinctive role in arguing the case for socialism and for winning people to these ideas. The commitment to class and democratic struggle in which the broadest possible alliances are built characterises Communist campaigning today in industry, in the social and public services, in communities and among people generally.

The party pursues a politics capable of attracting and involving the numbers of people who can bring about real change. But it needs crucially to find a new appeal and form of autonomous expression for young people, if its commitment to mass popular politics is to be sustained in practice.

In carrying forward its internationalist traditions of the common interest people have in fighting injustice and oppression, the party initiates campaigns in solidarity with the ANC and seeks support for the struggle of the PLO, the Sandinistas, the people of Chile and elsewhere. Central to this internationalist tradition is its involvement in the peace movement, a task made more possible by the disarmament initiatives of the Soviet Union. One of the party's urgent tasks in the wake of 1989 will be to take stock of the crisis within the world communist movement. One of the most exciting prospects at the start of the 1990s is the great possibility of healing the historic breach which has existed since 1917 between the communist and social-democratic traditions of the Left.

Despite its declining industrial infrastructure the party remains influential in the union movement. But its ability to renew itself will crucially depend on the extent to which its work, influence and strength in the labour movement can be increased. Throughout its history, though to a greatly varying extent, the party has sought a place within representative politics, through electoral work.

The present electoral system makes progress difficult. But the party needs to contest widely now as well as to campaign for electoral and constitutional reform. Communist representation can play a significant role in current struggles and in the pluralist socialist society of the future.

The ability of the Communist Party in a really significant way to make the contribution sketched out for it here is the big challenge now facing the party. It can be done by recognising that the restructuring of society and politics which is underway is of historic significance. The Communist Party cannot and should not want to escape its effects. It must confidently engage with them.

sustainable
development

The damage now being inflicted on our everyday and our global environment is a profound challenge to our ideas about progress, socialism, economic development and consumption. Without doubt, conflicts between economic practices and environmental protection, and between competing demands for shrinking resources, will continue to sharpen, not only for the next few decades, but for centuries to come.

It is no longer sufficient simply to add on pollution control and a bit of recycling to our existing programmes. We need to change our criteria for progress, for how we intend to achieve the global extinction of hunger, poverty and the threat of war.

The need to develop collective actions, both within and between nations to meet this enormous challenge, clearly contradicts Thatcherism's philosophy of regressive individualism.

There is already enough wealth production in Britain to provide decent housing and food, medical and social care, transport and communication, leisure and a pleasant stimulating environment for all our people, without further economic growth. We would have to make radical changes in the distribution and use of those resources. But even that is not enough. Today a 'sustainable economy in one country' is not possible. European and global changes are needed.

These changes must include severe new limits on pollution from industry, agriculture and transport; the banning of the most harmful products, such as CFCs, and research into alternatives; the use of taxation and other incentives to reduce harmful consumption and stimulate take-up of less damaging materials. Reducing traffic pollution will need new standards for producers, investment in public transport and the development of an integrated transport system.

A major redirection of technological research and development, and new, publicly declared techniques of economic assessment are needed which take into account environmental risks and renewal. So options like nuclear power which carry the risk, however small, of catastrophic environmental impacts, should be avoided, and extravagant use of finite resources, such as car fuel consumption, should be discouraged.

Economic choices should be aimed at conserving rather than depleting resources. The productivity of an assembly line can be measured by how many people it takes to make a product. But it can also be measured by its output of ill-health, accidents, stress and preventable diseases. These human measures of productivity must become as important as the commercial ones.

New forms of planning must be developed with the criterion of ecological renewal at their core. This will involve international regulatory organisation, the central and local state, as well as co-operation by consumers, community groups, companies, the green movement and political parties. Popular environmental forces must be found an enhanced role in political decision-making. New types of political institutions will be needed to pull together the popular and the professional.

The European Community should abandon the Common Agricultural Policy and introduce a new food policy to produce healthy, additive-free food, to minimise the chemical and energy inputs to agriculture, to preserve and improve our countryside and to provide fairer trading relations with poorer countries.

But just as important as these state and international interventions is change from below: individuals, households, communities and organisations working for a different ethic of consumption and lifestyle. This includes, but goes beyond, demands for unleaded petrol and ozone-friendly aerosols. It will involve choices about whether we spend our personal and our national surpluses on ever more consumer goods, or on more people-intensive benefits – culture, sport, public gardens, education and information, disabled access, health and social care of the young and old. If these latter benefits are given a cash value, then we might still talk of economic growth, but it would be a growth that involved a declining use of energy and resources, and ever reducing pollution.

In this culture, it would be as natural to opt for a shorter working life as today it is to opt for higher salaries. This would not be a romantic, backward-looking conservatism. It would need the exciting potential of information technology to decentralise and strengthen local control. Enhancement of the quality of our lives would include turning from centralised, large-scale production towards locally-owned and operated concerns.

Environmental considerations will affect any future conception of public ownership. Not only workers, but consumers, local residents, environmental groups, and world development lobbies should have a voice in the decision-making bodies of enterprises.

The arguments and the public support for the democratic control of multinational companies and other enterprises on environmental grounds are overwhelming. This democratic control might then be extended to tackle issues of training, equal opportunities, childcare, investment, the life-expectancy and renewability of products and so on.

The most explosive question for the sustainable future could be that of global inequality. The growing gap between rich and poor countries is both unjust and a major cause of instability and tension in the world. The burdens of world debt create an unavoidable link between international finance capital and economic development in poorer countries which promotes environmental despoliation. The squandering of human, financial and environmenal resources is in the very nature of unfettered free-market economic development. The destruction of the rainforests is part of a web of international economic relations. The average Briton consumes several score the amount of energy and raw materials used by an average Indian.

How can poorer peoples attain a standard of life comparable to that of 'developed' countries, without massively increasing global pollution and consumption? The West should not seek to impose alien values and cultures on the Third World, nor deny them access to the standard of living of the West.

The central criterion for tackling the global environmental crisis will be the development of new progressive, co-operative relationships between advanced nations and the developing world. Writing off the Third-World debt, and ending the dominating and exploitative relationship of the advanced nations over the Third World, thus relieving them of the crippling economic straitjacket which exacerbates environmental despoliation, will be part of the solution.

The international pooling of resources, the sharing of technological developments, the removal of ties to financial aid, the democratisation of the international economy, are areas where international co-operation must be developed. We must all recognise our mutual stake in world development.

This will inevitably require a major reassessment by people in the developed world of their own needs for material consumption to sustain their quality of life. Any sustainable development for Third World countries and the poorest strata of developed countries will involve global redistribution of resources from the better-off.

between and beyond
nations

There can be no progress for Britain which is not also part of a deep change in our country's relations with the rest of the world. The set of relationships, institutions and alliances that made up the postwar international settlement, based above all on the division of the world into East and West, are no longer sustainable.

One of the strategic aims of the 1990s should be a new progressive framework for the development of Britain's relations with Europe and the wider world. The history of Britain's faded dominance as a world economic, military, political and cultural power has produced a powerful paradox: a highly internationalised economy, within a web of international commitments inherited from its imperialist past; combined with a determined, defensive insularity.

A new set of pressures are bringing about a profound change in the relationship between the national and the international, which will remake international relations in the 1990s and beyond. This realignment demands a thorough reassessment of Britain's role in the world.

There are four overlapping forces behind this international realignment.

Globalisation

globalisation of economic relations, particularly through the growth of international companies, has been a persistent tendency since the 1950s. But the capitalist crisis of the 1970s gave it a new momentum. Combined with new technology it has paved the way for 24-hour-a-day global financial markets and much more integrated international production systems.

The integrity of the national economy as a distinct economic realm has virtually disappeared. The experience of the French socialists in 1981 shows it is almost impossible to sustain distinctive national economic policies successfully.

Globalisation is also changing the character and sovereignty of the nation state. The last twenty years have seen the growth of international companies and a proliferation of international agencies – the European Community, the International Monetary Fund and the United Nations – which in some way supplant the power of the nation state. Nowhere is this more keenly felt than in the non-industrialised countries, which have to bow to the world economic agenda.

This is creating pressures for realignment within nation states. Power is tending to move downwards as well as upwards. Localisation proceeds hand in hand with, and often as a response to, globalisation. Identities as a consequence are acquiring a new meaning. The most striking example of this in Britain is the rise of Scottish nationalism, which is besieging old notions of the British state and the British identity. The revived demand for Welsh national rights, and also for democratic power for English regions, although less prominent, is similarly significant.

Globalisation is affecting the whole notion of separate development of East and West. The idea of two separate, competing international economies, capitalist and socialist, has been undermined. The democratic revolutions of 1989 injected an urgency into a trend which was already developing towards increasing economic interaction, demanding a restructuring of international agencies, and new forms of co-operation and joint venture.

New Global Challenges

the second pressure for change is the growing recognition of the challenges now facing the whole of humanity. For the first time in human history, the possibility of the total destruction of the human race has become real: through nuclear holocaust or environmental and ecological catastrophe.

At the same time the division in the world between the haves and the have-nots is growing. The waste of resources on arms production and military preparations is in itself a main contributor to the global problems of poverty, famine and backwardness. And debt, trade, development, control and use of finite resources, together with scientific and technological development, put intolerable strains on the world economy which can only be met by a new global settlement.

These global challenges call for a truly revolutionary transformation of relations between peoples, states and regions. It means increased importance for democratically controlled and representative agencies: a wholesale restructuring of the UN, World Bank and IMF.

And we need a new understanding of sovereignty: an international system that combines respect for the legitimate sovereign rights of countries and peoples with an acceptable and enforceable system of international financial and economic regulation.

The Break-up of the Superpower World

the third pressure for international realignment is the break-up of the bipolar superpower world of the cold war. Above all, Gorbachev's foreign policy has transformed international understanding and possibilities. Gorbachev heralds the break-up of the old binary blocs and the stagnant mentality which went with them. The Soviet Union has reassessed its political approach and abandoned its strategy of military intervention in the Third World. The upheavals in Eastern Europe make it impossible to talk any longer of a homogeneous Eastern bloc.

Meanwhile Gorbachev has created the momentum for a process of nuclear disarmament and made the first moves to open up the Soviet Union's relations with the Far East. The Soviet Union is looking outwards, to integrate itself within the international economy. In parallel Gorbachev is promoting a new internationalism of co-operation, co-development and humanism building on concepts advanced by some developing countries, peace movements and non-aligned governments.

Britain's postwar foreign and defence policy rested on being a senior partner in the NATO bloc as part of a common Western defence against an ever-present threat of Soviet tanks rolling across West Germany. If these trends continue Britain will need entirely new ground rules for its foreign policy in the 1990s, underpinned by conventional and nuclear disarmament, an end to military blocs, an enlarged role for the UN and promotion of peace.

This will mark an epochal shift: a final laying-to-rest of the prewar Bolshevik threat, and the postwar cold war ideology, which have so dominated and distorted international relations. It will open up radical new possibilities for progressive international politics.

Europe

the fourth pressure transforming the world and Britain's place within it is Europeanisation. This is not a new trend, but it has gained renewed momentum with the 1992 EC integration programme. However, the process is not confined to the EC. Perestroika in the USSR has unleashed in turn the most extraordinary series of upheavals in Eastern Europe which completely transform the possibilities for a common European home.

Response

International issues are becoming much more important in British politics. Thatcherism's regressive response, playing upon the paradox of insular chauvinism and economic openness, is strategically vulnerable to a concerted challenge. The Left and progressive forces will not mount that challenge if they remain stuck within the political demarcation lines of the old world, broadly accepting imperialist attitudes or taking a moral rather than political stand on internationalism.

The trajectory of Britain's international development into the next century should be set by a progressive international settlement. This will combine several core components.

At its heart will be a new division between national and international politics. The labour process involved in the multinational production and assembly of products across Europe will require far greater co-operation, exchange and joint activity between trade unions on a European and a world level.

The problem of controlling international companies must be dealt with at a national level through regulation and, where possible, social ownership. But this would be of limited value if it was not backed by moves towards international regulation. Stricter controls over the City of London will have limited effect without a new approach to international monetary reform.

Central to a new international outlook is a progressive role for Britain within Europe. Britain's membership of the EC is a reality which must define the way we conceive of our future. The EC is the means through which West European capital is restructuring, creating a single market and setting up an area of exchange rate stability. Its aim is to protect and develop European industry, research and technology. Other European countries are increasingly affected by EC development and defining their relationship with it. We need to give the meaning of Europeanism a wider and more democratic content.

The British labour movement and progressive forces, in co-operation with the continental Left, need to formulate a programme for a social Europe involving minimum standards for training, unemployment relief, health and safety, pensions, working time, involvement in corporate decision-making, and higher environmental standards. A range of alliances can be formed with continental forces, both left and right, to press for such a programme. We should be under no illusion that as things stand at present the idea of social Europe, let alone the practice of it, is highly underdeveloped. Nor should that struggle become a substitute for action to achieve progressive arrangements and legislation in Britain.

Moving in this direction will mean more power is transferred to Brussels. It will therefore be essential to democratise the European Community institutions. The European Commission needs to be accountable to the European Parliament. At the moment, decision-making is shrouded in bureaucracy, secrecy and opaqueness. It must be made open and transparent at both a national and European level. The present democratic deficit is chronic.

The expansion of the EC to incorporate poorer European nations like Malta, Cyprus and Turkey, means that the Community is likely to become less of a club for the rich nations of Western Europe. Combined with the differing impact Europeanisation will have on poor regions within nations, this calls for a redistributive regional settlement within Europe.

The EC is likely to become a key focus for Britain's relations with Eastern Europe. The opening-up of Eastern Europe creates new possibilities for co-operative economic and cultural relations: the creation of a common European home which includes Prague as naturally as it includes Paris. We need a new vision of Europe, one without nuclear weapons, one in which West and East live and co-operate together, and one which is not divided into two military blocs.

Europeanisation carries with it considerable risks and costs.

It is already leading to widespread industrial restructuring, job losses and further concentration of economic power. It could be used to turn the EC into the foundations for a new military bloc, with a regressive, defensive approach to non-Europe. These risks mean it is more important than ever for progressive politics to engage with Europeanisation.

Britain should also seek a more co-operative relationship with the developing world, both independently and through the EC. It should become part of a wider movement in the advanced world for a new international economic order. But such a new order has be to influenced by Third World nations, who should not be regarded as passive recipients of whatever aid the advanced world chooses to hand to them.

Some of the themes of a new North-South settlement would be a moratorium on debt, a new deal for primary producers, and a much higher level of development aid. It would also explicitly accept people's rights to political and economic self-determination.

International solidarity with liberation struggles and movements remains a responsibility. But progressive movements and parties need to develop a wider conception of solidarity, which includes support for indigenous peoples, environmental and resource campaigns, struggles over debt, trade, aid and development.

Finally, the foundations for traditional left-right positions on defence and disarmament are being uprooted. An historic opportunity is emerging for Britain to contribute to a new era in international disarmament. Western defence policies based on the 'looming Soviet threat' are no longer credible.

Britain's priority should be to contribute to the rolling process of disarmament set in train by Gorbachev. The striking thing about his initiatives is that they make disarmament possible through a variety of routes. Unilateralism has been made real by Gorbachev's own moves. But he has also lent a new respectability to multilateralism and bilateralism, by demonstrating that meaningful disarmament can proceed through negotiation. Britain has a special responsibility here as one of the main exporters of armaments and spenders on arms production.

What is striking about these international developments is that Thatcherism is so vulnerable, defending an outmoded international role for Britain, as evidenced by, for instance, her chauvinistic clinging to Britain's 'independent nuclear deterrent' and determination to modernise it with Trident. That fear of the future is a sure sign of strategic weakness.

But if progressive forces are to take advantage of that weakness, two things are essential. They need to map out a new ideological perspective based on the achievement of new strategic settlements for Britain's role in the world – covering relations with Europe, the developing world and disarmament. That in turn needs to be underpinned by the spread of a new progressive international humanism, which is capable of embracing internationalisation confidently.

Ireland

One of the greatest tests of our ability to construct a new internationalism will be whether British opinion can respond in new ways to the long-running Irish crisis. Striking out on a new path in relations between the British and the Irish opens up exciting prospects for a joint exploration of new types of links between peoples.

Fundamental to this must be a recognition of the Irish people's right to self-determination. The failure to enable people in Ireland actually to exercise this right is what lies behind the continuing crisis in Northern Ireland. The complexity, uniqueness and closeness of relations between our peoples, however, marks out that crisis from other, simply colonial ones. The divisions and contradictions within and around Northern Ireland form a complex web which will not be easily undone or resolved.

Everyone concerned with democratic progress in Britain itself needs to face up to the issue of Ireland. If the viability of mass political action is not demonstrated in relation to Ireland, then those who choose violence will continue to win sufficient support to perpetuate their self-defeating campaigns.

A central challenge in building a new politics in Britain will be the generation of a new approach and involvement around the Irish question. New trends in and around Ireland will influence how this happens: the deep sense of frustration within Northern Ireland at the continuation of the crisis and the desire on the part of many political forces, particularly among Republicans, to explore new ways forward; the shift in interest on the part of British governments from Belfast and Unionism to Dublin and the government of the Irish Republic. The latter is the starting point for the Anglo-Irish Agreement which, for all its great weaknesses, does ensure that the issues of repression in Northern Ireland have been internationalised.

Beyond and above all these are the changes, only now beginning to be felt, which derive from Britain and Ireland's joint membership of the European Community. These will have a profound long-term impact. Although in many ways, particularly in the economy, that impact will be negative, EC membership will increasingly deprive London of its dominant role in Irish politics and focus attention on the need for and possibility of all-Ireland approaches on a wide range of social and economic concerns.

There needs to be a positive programme to eradicate the inheritance of centuries of British domination and provide a basis upon which a new Irish nationhood can be constructed. The following general themes are crucial:

– A future British government should declare its intention to create the political, social and economic conditions in which the Irish people can exercise their right to self-determination.

– Action by a British government must enable progressive political forces in Ireland to win over many of those currently committed to Unionist and reactionary ideas.

– There is an urgent need to establish a regime of justice and security in Northern Ireland in place of the present 'law and order' approach, including economic, security and legal measures to provide full equality of opportunity for Catholics.

– Both London and the EC should make a long-term and substantial economic commitment to the Irish economy as a whole, with an immediate crash programme of publicly funded investment to overcome the inheritance of poverty, deindustrialisation and discrimination.

– Achievement of progressive harmonisation of law, social, economic and governmental practices on an all-Ireland basis.

– The exploration of new structures of democratic accountability for the people of Northern Ireland through which they can influence those economic and social decisions currently exercised by London or Brussels.

The development of dialogue with all in Ireland interested in working towards a peaceful, united future.

new times, *new economy*

The strategic aim of progressive politics in the 1990s must be to establish a new consensus over how the economy should develop, based on a new relationship between social need and efficiency.

This will require a new division of responsibilities between national government and international agencies, between the central state and autonomous social organisations, between planning bodies and private enterprise. In the medium term, the aim should be to establish a new definition of the mixed economy, which goes well beyond a mix between public and private ownership.

Goals

There are four main aims of progressive modernisation. Firstly, it should be sustainable. It should sustain people, providing them with the skills, confidence and security to engage in productive work. It should also establish a new approach to working time which would balance the demands of production and the needs of the domestic sphere in caring for dependents and children. It should sustain efficiency, through a major investment in the foundations of the modern economy, research and development, skills and education.

It should sustain the environment. Wasteful and unnecessary products which deplete natural resources and which often have their origin in the despoliation of the Third World must be phased out. Environmental safety should be written into production and products as an integral goal. Energy policy in particular needs to aim at sustainable development.

Secondly, it should be a democratic modernisation, expanding popular control over economic decisions within the workplace, locally, nationally and through international regulatory institutions.

Thirdly, it should establish a new ethic of progressive consumerism. Consumption is highly political, as recent campaigns over the quality of food, transport safety and the future of the NHS have shown. But it is also highly personal, individualised, a way in which most people feel able to express themselves and say something about their lives. Consumer politics offers an important link between the individual and the collective.

Thatcherism's consumerism stresses relatively passive market purchases of bundles of goods. Progressive consumerism should be about providing people with more time free from work to develop a whole range of pursuits, interests and qualities.

Fourthly, the elements must cohere into a new idea of the public interest, which accepts that social interests are made up of an amalgam of constantly conflicting aspirations. Producers and consumers, men and women, do not have the same interests or needs which can be measured by the same yardstick. The social interest will not be fully represented purely through strategies to control ownership and production. It must also be present in approaches to consumption.

Means

achieving these goals will require sweeping changes in who makes decisions and how they are made. The state – local and national – and European and international regulatory bodies, will play a vital role in promoting these changes. But state measures will not succeed unless they work in tandem with changes from within society. The achievement of the medium-term goals we have outlined implies much more than a sudden burst of legislation: it will require a 'socialisation' of economic decision-making.

The key to that will be the erosion and break-up of unaccountable concentrations of economic power. Yet history tells us that such changes are bound to meet widespread resistance from sections of the City, business, the multinationals and parts of the state.

So what are the means to bring about these goals we have outlined from within society?

Trade-Union Bargaining: the contribution of the trade-union movement to progressive social and economic change will depend on three key factors. Firstly, after ten years of anti-trade-union legislation, there needs to be a positive legal framework for organised labour. Secondly, the union movement has to revitalise itself to play a strategic but independent, political campaigning role; and thirdly, trade unions must win the public over to a modernised view of them as organisations capable of making a real contribution to the quality of life.

The declining numbers of young people entering the labour market in the 1990s are creating an historic opportunity for unions to win strategic gains for women. Thus a major agenda should be to press for production to be oriented more around the needs of women and domestic work, through childcare facilities, more flexible working time, career breaks with guaranteed jobs at the end, women's training and career advice.

It should also become the daily bread-and-butter of trade-union negotiations to ensure that workplaces are adapted to the needs of workers with disabilities and that black workers have just as much access to job opportunities as white workers.

Technology and intensified competition is putting a premium on skills. Major advances in skills training, through individual annual entitlements for workers or company training plans, should be a strategic union goal for the next few years.

Employers are increasingly seeking to reorganise working time – around seven-day production, longer, flexible shifts etc – to make greater use of expensive new technology in manufacturing or to provide more comprehensive consumer services. The unions must meet this employers' agenda with pressure to reduce and reorganise working time to suit workers' needs. Unions could, for instance, press for long-term deals to include employment security clauses in exchange for more flexible working practices.

The Green Movement presents perhaps the most powerful rising challenge to current social and economic priorities. Increasing numbers of people are identifying with the broad movement challenging the freedom to pollute, contaminate and exploit our finite global resources. However green political parties and trade unions become, there remains a need for a movement which will put the planet and the environment first; mobilising opinion and exerting pressure through consumer power, on commercial and industrial exploitation, and promoting alternative lifestyles and principles for a more equitable global share of resources.

Local Campaigns: for instance, the campaign to defend the Scottish coal and steel industries, local anti-takeover campaigns and the strategies being developed by modernising Labour local authorities, could prove very powerful in drawing a wide cross-section of people into the politics of local democracy and economic development. These local campaigns are important examples of how new broad coalitions for progressive economic restructuring could shape up.

Consumer Campaigns: the defence of health services, protest at BT's poor performance, transport safety and food hygiene rows, are all indicative of how politicised consumption is becoming. Consumer campaigns command widespread support, both from well-off and badly-off; from rail users to phone subscribers. But they also attack the unaccountable nature of economic decisions. In the consumer goods and services sector, key decisions about production are increasingly taken 'close to the consumer' and influenced by market and retail considerations. We have seen an encouraging increase in consumers' influence over the market through demand and choice, demonstrating the possibilities of gaining some progressive levers in the market itself.

Information to the consumer at the point of retail is highly significant in influencing choices, such as in the statutory labelling of packaged foodstuffs for example. The sharply competitive market will be very sensitive to consumer choice, including by consumer boycott.

Anti-Privatisation Campaigns: opposition to water and electricity privatisation and compulsory competitive tendering campaigns, for example, could also build support for different policies. These campaigns should provide the labour movement with an outstanding opportunity to campaign against privatisation in alliance with consumers, to stand for the wider social interest while representing the interests of workers.

Anti-Inequality Campaigns over the poll tax, in defence of child benefit and against further tax cuts will also be important in reproducing broad support for more egalitarian policies. They are vital both materially, to the people hardest hit by these changes, but also ideologically, in contesting Thatcherism's reactionary economic values.

All these are areas where popular pressure can be developed towards a more progressive economic agenda. Such an economic strategy would revolve around refashioned divisions between local, national and international initiatives; planning and markets; macro- and micro-economic policies. But at the heart of these changes must be a challenge to the overweening power of privately owned companies, which dominate economic decision-making in this country.

Local, National and International

key decisions affecting Britain's economy are taken in the headquarters of transnational corporations. Many of these companies control wealth greater than that of entire nations, yet are hierarchically controlled and highly exploitative of the world's resources, making enormous profits from cheap labour, and helping to prop up oppressive regimes. Their ability to move production to countries where taxation is low and labour is cheap undermines living standards and trade-union rights, and diminishes the ability of governments and nations to shape their own economies and futures.

Some of these transnationals are British owned, but increasingly they are from Japan, Korea, continental Europe and the USA. Progressive development will be impossible unless they are effectively regulated and influenced by both national and international bodies. This will be no easy task. Changes in corporate power, including sub-contracting, international joint ventures, franchising and licensing agreements, have made economic power more complex and opaque. It needs to be approached with realism rather than slogans. But it must be tackled.

And a distinction can usefully be made between those transnationals which are linked in with the international division of labour, such as ICL or General Motors, and the financial conglomerates such as BAT, Hanson, and Lonrho, with their diverse interests. Steps could be taken to break up the latter with their excessive concentrations of wealth and economic power, and to minimise the uncontrolled flow of wealth from one country to another.

Any strategy to control transnational companies will have to work at several different levels. There is no single lever that can be pulled to bring about the changes we seek.

What is needed is a new, progressive and modernising internationalism which has socially regulated and responsible transnational companies as part of our global, interdependent future. The struggle to attain this will have to be worldwide – transnationals control about 50 per cent of world trade and over 70 per cent of the marketing of basic export products from the underdeveloped countries. We in Britain will have to play a constructive part, instead of putting a brake, as at present, on all international initiatives.

Local Strategies: the deep-rooted and longstanding regional inequalities in the UK economy have been greatly aggravated by the destruction of traditional economic activity, particularly in the period 1979-81. The development of sunrise industries – information technology and new electronics – has been clearly concentrated in specific regions, and the booming financial services sector has lent a further selective stimulus to growth, most notably in the south-east.

At the same time, local authorities have had their room for manoeuvre curtailed by central government where new capital projects for local economic development are concerned. The Urban Development Corporations have still to demonstrate their capacity for an economic regeneration which increases local employment and sustains local communities. Yet they have an effective stranglehold on the development of major economic projects and employment training.

New investment mechanisms need to be established, through development agencies, financial institutions and local regulatory bodies to promote new businesses and local economic regeneration. Thus, for instance, a 'green bank' might be established to fund businesses specialising in recycling or developing environmentally safe products. Local authorities should be given greatly expanded economic roles. This would make strategic planning more democratic and more effective. For it is at the level of the town and the city that communities confront international capital in the shape of inward investment.

Local resources to bargain with capital need to be

expanded to pressurise companies to meet social obligations. All public bodies should be required to set up procedures to ensure compliance with contract and equal opportunity clauses.

National Strategies: these can be pursued through a variety of routes. Social ownership will be a vital component, with the government taking a leading role in the development of the new technological and communications infrastructure, and holding special stakes in key utilities and corporations. But it will also come about through collective funds for workers and consumers. For instance, trade unions, the green movement and local authorities could co-operate to establish 'green stakes' in major polluters. Consumer collective funds could be set up for utility companies. Moves towards social ownership will only win popular support if that ownership brings tangible decision-making power, rather than the pretence of power offered by the Thatcherite strategy of sales of small batches of company shares to private individuals.

In addition, there needs to be a much stronger regulatory framework for entire sectors of the economy, as different as food processing and finance. These regulatory bodies could set standards for local content in production, employment policies, ecological safety, product quality and safety. They should have the power to award refunds, discounts, or deny companies access to the market until they have improved their performance. There needs to be much tighter control over mergers and takeovers, with the onus on the acquirer to prove the benefit of the decision according to social as well as commercial criteria.

Local authorities and devolved national assemblies could play a crucial role in this regulatory system, to ensure regulation is guided by democratic imperatives and retains popular support. In addition, consideration should be given to establishing democratic bodies to be the focus for complaints.

In addition, national strategies must control the export of capital and should aim to lessen the UK economy's dependence on foreign multinationals by promoting indigenous development, especially in niche markets where Britain could establish an international specialisation.

European Strategies: in the 1990s the key points to influence competition between transnational companies will be the local level – in the towns where these companies invest – but also the

European level. The aim should be to establish high European standards to regulate investment by and competition between transnationals. These standards should cover workers' individual and collective rights. This needs to be combined with a concerted European regional industrial policy to prevent economic power drifting to a Europe dominated by the powerful West German economy.

Moves towards international forms of social ownership, between state, unions, local authorities in different countries, need to be developed to match the internationalised power of big corporations.

International Strategies: these will be vital as all the major industrial capitalist economies are becoming more integrated. The industrialisation of China, India and Brazil, combined with the opening of the East European and Soviet economies will hasten this process still further.

A new positive approach to supranational, supra-regional regulation and planning is needed. Developing countries have long been arguing for a new international economic order which would require co-ordinated intervention to remould world markets. A progressive British government should develop that approach, which might include the following steps:

– Joining the European Monetary System and working for European monetary union in the long run. This would help to stabilise the pound and prevent large speculative currency flows. A new central bank should be established which would be democratically controlled.

– An international conference – including the Soviet Union and industrialising countries – should be convened to establish a new international monetary order: a Bretton Woods financial settlement for the 1990s.

– The moves by General Agreement on Tariffs and Trade to open the EC to products from developing countries and eliminate dumping by EC states into developing countries should be supported.

– Undertaking joint ventures with East European and developing countries to promote more co-operative pan-regional economic integration.

Markets and Planning

a progressive economic strategy will need to use both planning and market mechanisms to achieve its objectives.

The market is a useful tool to co-ordinate lots of decentralised economic decisions. Markets can provide incentives and discipline, and promote innovation, flexibility and diversity. But some goods such as education and health should not be provided through the market's criteria of ability to pay. And the experience of the Thatcher years is now making it abundantly clear that balanced economic development will require the social ownership of basic utilities, energy production and distribution, means of transport and telecommunications.

Moreover, market-based decisions about investment are frequently very short-sighted and even those which determine the immediate availability of goods are considered in very narrow terms, neglecting the impact of current decisions on the future shape of the economy. Above all, the market economy in Britain works to reinforce inequalities in economic power, which means that economic decisions reflect the priorities and interests of the rich, well-off and powerful.

For these reasons strategic planning will be vital to set the economy's dynamic path of development, through investment in research and development, training and skills. Planning is an everyday economic tool. Consumers use it, for instance, to plan holidays. Companies use it extensively within their organisation to plan production. It will be needed to restore and renew our ravaged infrastructural industries, such as coal and steel. Or to meet people's environmental and safety concerns over transport, by providing modern, integrated transport systems.

But planning also has serious limitations. Firstly, it is difficult to collect all the information needed to plan accurately, especially during a period of economic restructuring and intense international competitive pressure. Secondly, planning has often seen the national economy as an integrated unit, like an enormous factory. In an internationalising economy, national planning will be less effective.

Thirdly, planning has often been elitist. It needs to be more popularly based in democratic decision-making, whether locally through councils, or nationally through regulatory bodies or assemblies. And fourthly, planning has sometimes been spectacularly inefficient, as in the East European states. It has neither ensured that consumer demands are met, nor that their economies have been modernised.

The vital thing is how to combine planning and markets, private and public decisions. Many of the most successful capitalist economies – Japan, Sweden and South Korea – use planning. But they use it in conjunction with the market. Their aim is to make strategic, planned interventions in markets, to influence the outcome of market decisions. They do not attempt to plan to the last detail every outcome that will emerge from the market.

Planning is often based on past information about economic performance, extrapolated into the future. Market decisions are often confined just to current choices. Both approaches are inadequate to cope with the uncertainty and rapid shifts in the economy of the new times. A strategic approach to economic development will require a new combination of market and plan.

Macro and Micro

new divisions must be established between macro-economic policy – governing public spending, borrowing, interest rates and the exchange rate – and micro-economic policy – covering the nuts and bolts of the economy (production, investment and training). This division between the macro and the micro largely corresponds to another: between the financial and the productive. A progressive modernisation should develop the productive economy by protecting it from the speculative flow of international financial capital.

The management of the exchange rate and interest rates is particularly important, as these are the key links between the British economy and international markets. Britain should join the EMS and press for international monetary reform. For it is only within a new international framework that Britain will be insulated from speculative financial flows.

Although Keynesian policies of demand management to promote full employment have lost their potency, macro-economic policy is still important in promoting and channelling growth. An expansionary programme targeted at the public sector, the infrastructure and services such as education and health is a much more effective strategic use of public spending than tax cuts which fuel imports.

In tandem, progressive modernisation would turn on a new approach to investment in training and employment. Central to an economic strategy would be the reorganisation of working time over the week, year and life. More flexible forms of retirement, sabbaticals, career breaks for men and women, more flexible working time for parents with young children, a shorter working day or week – all will be on the agenda in the 1990s. With the benefit of technology, overall reductions in working time could significantly contribute to the goal of full employment.

But beyond that a progressive modernisation should provide a universal guarantee of employment or training, through offering everyone unemployed a place on a high-quality training and economic development programme, which would link investment in skills to the creation of jobs. Employment training is currently proving to be a failure, with only one-third take-up, and a large number of people leaving schemes before completion. The skills of British workers will be vital to their security and prosperity in the 1990s. Britain needs a sustained high-quality approach to training through life.

the **social** *society*

Central to progressive change in the 1990s must be a new social cohesion, a social settlement between the 'insiders' and the 'outsiders' of British society, to end the savage inequality of the two-thirds/one-third society created by Thatcherism's reactionary restructuring. It should involve a new approach to childcare, health, education, housing and the rights and resources of the elderly. The starting point for this new social agenda is to examine the three key reasons why the traditional role of the welfare state has been undermined in the last two decades.

Firstly, the postwar welfare state was designed for a world of male full employment and female unpaid domestic and caring work within the nuclear family. But social and economic change has thrown up new social needs which the welfare state has been ill-equipped to meet. For instance, female lone parents now constitute one of the fastest-growing groups dependent on the welfare state.

Secondly, the inflexibility, paternalism and bureaucracy of the welfare state provoked mounting criticism in the 1970s. Thatcherism articulated this discontent from the Right, with an attack on public spending and the public sector in general. But community and service-consumer groups, women's organisations and the voluntary sector also mounted sustained attacks on the poor standards of quality, service and choice.

Thirdly, the passage to new times is also creating new ideas of what welfare and wellbeing amount to. The postwar welfare state developed around benefits, delivered by professionals, to relatively passive claimants. The new ideas stress a wider quality of life beyond a package of benefits, with greater stress on the importance of positive choice, quality and control. A new social agenda for the 1990s cannot be based upon piecemeal reform: it requires a thorough rethinking of the principles for a welfare system to match the new times. At its core will be a new division of labour between the state and society, experts and people, the collective and the individual, need and efficiency.

State and Society

the starting point should be to look directly at social needs in the 1990s and then work out how best they should be met. Social needs have become more complex and diverse, as the workforce has become more segmented, the traditional family has declined, and social aspirations have expanded.

A new welfare system must have the flexibility to respond to a plurality of social needs, which will make the development of democratic structures essential. Welfare services could, for example, be governed nationally and locally by bodies made up of a diverse representation of interest groups.

However, social needs have become more pressing and intense with the growth of poverty and inequality. Flexibility in the delivery of welfare has to be matched by a determined strategy to redistribute resources.

The state must play the key role in developing that overall strategy. It should also ensure high standards of delivery are maintained. But the central state is ill-equipped to provide a wide range of flexible services. So properly regulated sub-contracting to co-operatives, voluntary organisations and self-help groups, to provide housing management or childcare services, for instance, should be a key part of a new welfare strategy. The aim is that change is embedded in the way people live, rather than enshrined in the procedures of the state.

For instance, part of a new health policy should be to envelop the NHS in a wider web of health services: in the workplace, through self-help groups, community health centres, health education and preventive health care. A new politics of food production and consumption, which could be taken up by consumer groups and trade unions in collective bargaining, should be part of that agenda.

The Collective and the Individual

a new welfare agenda must involve a new relationship between collective responsibility and individual choice.

Collective finance for welfare will remain crucial if people's life chances are not to be left to the vagaries of the market or the inequalities of background and inheritance. Radical reform of the tax and benefit system, possibly through the introduction of a basic income for all citizens, and a local income tax to replace the poll tax, should be a central part of a social strategy for the 1990s.

In addition there needs to be greater stress on expanding individual choice, rights and entitlements. Poverty is not a problem of the poor alone. Its existence shapes our relationships in all spheres of life and creates tensions and divisions within and across families, neighbourhoods and regions. A new welfare strategy will only redistribute towards the poor if it can win the support of the well-off. To win that support the stress needs to be on universal rather than targeted benefits.

Significantly, those parts of the welfare state which have retained greatest public support, such as the NHS and child benefit, combine universal individual entitlements with collective finance. Universal entitlements to a minimum income, pensions, care for the elderly and childcare, could command similarly widespread support.

This universalism needs to be combined with greater individual choice to allow people to tailor services more to their needs. A new welfare strategy could deliver a wide range of universal entitlements to health care, post-school education and housing, for people to use as best suits their needs. For instance, a programme of care and support for the elderly should cover health, housing, pensions, income-support and retirement policies. The elements of this policy must then be tailored to specific and differing needs, as defined by the elderly people themselves and their organisations.

Experts and People

the provision of highly skilled advice and expertise to people who could not afford to buy such help through the market is another strength of the welfare state. Yet one of the main consumer criticisms, for instance in education, is that professional priorities predominate over the views of consumers – children and parents.

Building on positive examples of professional commitment – schools where great care is taken to inform and involve parents, medical practices which are flexible and responsive – we need to

create more open and egalitarian relationships between the professionals of the welfare state and the people they serve.

The starting point should be to abandon the postwar welfare
state's idea of all claimants as passive, relatively powerless clients in
need of help, while not abandoning the seriously sick, elderly or very
young to the vagaries of unsupported 'community care'. A modernising welfare strategy should hold that people are capable of taking
control of their lives, playing a role in shaping and delivering
services. For instance, in a participatory health agenda people
would take more control of their health through self-help initiatives on
diet, health education and promotion, exercise and self-diagnosis,
as well as having provision or financial support for a wider range of
treatments including 'alternative medicine'.

One of the most striking examples of this approach is the way
that women who have faced male violence have established
women's refuges based on self-help and mutual support, in alliance
with local authorities. This creative approach to welfare has had
much wider ramifications, forcing the legal profession and police to
be more aware of women's demands. It is a form of welfare which is
contributing to a wider social change.

Another example is the way that the AIDS crisis has been
constructively confronted by mutual help and support groups
among those with HIV or AIDS conditions, working in alliance with
the NHS or voluntary agencies.

Needs and Efficiency

as things stand, welfare needs and services are primarily defined
by bureaucratic procedures, which are in turn determined by
financial constraints and a management imperative of efficiency as
value for money.

It is essential that a new strategy should start from a much
more open assessment of need. So, in education, a democratically
determined national curriculum should be the alternative to the
authoritarian curriculum being imposed by the government. In the
case of the NHS, there needs to be a much wider debate about the
nation's health priorities. In both cases the detail of provision also
needs to be worked out more democratically, to establish the best
way of meeting particular needs within schools and hospitals.

This democratic audit of need should be the foundation for efficient management. Large parts of the public sector are severely underfunded. But funding is neither the sole cause nor the entire solution to the problems of the welfare state. The public sector, like much of industry, has been badly managed. A new strategy must involve better management to ensure resources are used in the most effective way. Good management is essential to show people that their tax contributions are being well used, and thereby maintain public support for welfare.

Take two examples of how the principles of this new strategy for welfare might work in practice: housing and childcare.

Housing

housing is both a primary human need and a collective national asset. Houses are the foundations for most people's private, individual worlds. But they usually outlast the people who live in them. They are part of the collective resources of society. Housing policy needs to aim at satisfying the varied needs of the current generation, while also preserving and improving our housing stock for future generations.

Housing debates have traditionally been preoccupied with tenure: renting versus owning, thereby squeezing from the agenda issues like homelessness, housing conditions and cost. Central to a new policy approach will be four considerations: access, cost, quality and control.

Homelessness is a major and growing problem, particularly for the young, for single people and the poor. An end to homelessness and the misery of substandard housing must be the top priority, not least by strengthening and widening the scope of legal protection for the homeless.

Access to housing is, however, often determined by cost. The system of collective housing finance and subsidy needs to be radically reformed. Ideally a universal housing allowance would be paid to mortgage-holders and tenants alike, designed to concentrate resources on the lowest income grouping.

This individual entitlement should allow people more choice over their housing. Housing provision should meet the diversity of needs: between different age groups, between the childless and those with children, between men and women. It should be possible to plan provision according to demographic shifts, such as in the current projections for the increase in elderly; for whom the housing implications are substantial, not least in terms of the special requirements of disability. The special housing problems of rural areas, particularly those areas subject to immigration for retirement and the purchase of holiday homes, are another example where attention should be targeted.

This will require new relationships between experts – such as planners and architects – and users. But it will also require a new approach for central and local government in establishing and policing standards.

Councils and other public housing agencies should become strategic actors in the housing field as well as providers and managers of rented housing. This could allow them to become potentially liberating bodies for greater control by tenants and home-owners alike.

Both home-owners and council tenants face delays and poor-quality maintenance work from small builders and direct labour organisations. Councils could develop their direct labour organis-ations through internal competition or sub-contracting so that they provided high-quality services to tenants but also to home-owners at a fee.

Local authorities should in principle also move into the private housing market, with estate agencies for tenants seeking to move, by buying property in the private sector, and by strengthened powers to enforce standards in the private rented sector and boarding houses. A new charter of tenants' rights should guarantee private tenants' security and peaceful occupation of their homes.

Housing can provide a focus for the self-managing society with the transfer of large concentrations of stock in local authority control to community-based organisations and the development of repairs and management co-operatives for owners.

Childcare

because Thatcherism's philosophy sees children as a purely family responsibility, social support for child-rearing has dismally failed to keep pace with the rise in women's paid employment and changing patterns of household size and lifestyles.

The lack of childcare support in Britain will be a major issue in the 1990s. The state needs to take a strategic role in setting targets and standards for provision, including the educational, emotional and social needs of children, and ensuring sufficient public finance is available. There should be a universal entitlement to childcare for all parents, including the option for a carer's benefit.

However, childcare services will only meet the diversity of needs of different parents, with different jobs, and children of differing ages, if it is delivered in a flexible, responsive way based on regulation of standards. That means ensuring a range of provision, from employer-funded workplace nurseries, to those run by the voluntary sector, co-operatives, regulated childminders (suitably trained, better paid and with career prospects), more extensive use of school buildings and properly funded informal solutions among networks of parents.

The creation of the service would be in the hands of those who use it and so would stand a good chance of meeting their needs efficiently. The state, collective finance, and expert advice would play a supportive, enabling role.

The extension of childcare provision would appeal across the classes of working women and would build a new coalition for an expansion of welfare. But it would disproportionately benefit the least well-off. It would amount to the biggest attack on family poverty since the introduction of child benefit. It would help to free women from the burdens of their double shift in work at home and in employment, and contribute to a social and cultural reformation of relations between men and women.

political **settlement**

A new political settlement is an essential element of any new political vision. The present political order is undoubtedly one of the most regressive features of both Thatcherism and British society.

Thatcherism has introduced a degree of authoritarianism into British civic and political life that is quite unique. But it has only been able to do this because of its ruthless exploitation of the peculiarly undeveloped nature of our democracy.

We have a profoundly undemocratic electoral system which has meant that every single government since the war has been elected on a minority of the votes cast. And once that government is in office, its powers are enormous. There is no separation of powers in Britain's unwritten constitution. There is no president, no representative second chamber nor system of regional government – all features which exist in other Western countries. Parliamentary sovereignty means that the government of the day enjoys enormous power with few constraints.

We live in a country dominated by perhaps the most centralised system in Western Europe. Members of our society are regarded as subjects not citizens: their rights are not enshrined in any written constitution independent of the parliamentary majority of the day. This unreformed state undermines democracy and civil liberties.

It is therefore totally inadequate to see the post-Thatcherite era in terms of a return to 1979, or for that matter 1945. A much more fundamental reform of the British constitution is required, along the lines of the popular initiative of Charter 88, calling for a written constitution, a bill of rights and open government: demands which are central to any progressive socialist renewal.

We are moving into an era in which the possibilities for pluralism and self-determination are much greater than ever before. More than that, there has been an enormous expansion of civil society in the postwar period. That process is likely to accelerate. What is needed is a state form which can creatively interact with civil society, which is enabling rather than disabling.

We need a new kind of constitutional settlement, although

we recognise that its terms will certainly evolve with time and external events, such as any move towards a European federalism.

Our first aim must be the enhancement of democracy on all fronts, nationally, regionally, and locally. The electoral system must be reformed, with the primary aim of replacing the present first-past-the-post system with proportional representation. This would mean that everyone's vote would be democratically represented in parliament, unlike at present. We recognise this would generally mean some form of coalition government, but it would be more representative of popular opinion than is the present system. Indeed, it is positively desirable because, compared with the present system, it would require different political forces to co-operate and so foster interaction of different political traditions.

The Labour Party clings to the view that to consider proportional representation would be a diversion from the necessary task of winning the next general election. This belief fails to recognise how far the experience of the last ten years has thrown the archaic, authoritarian and unrepresentative nature of our parliamentary system into especially stark relief.

The Labour Party's continuing view that it has the democratic right to exercise a political counter-monopoly against Thatcherism represents a radical failure of democratic and socialist vision and a very short-term assessment of political realities. The Labour Party's own current project, as outlined in its policy review, relies upon a considerable flourishing of democratic activity and widespread decentralisation of political power.

A system of PR would begin to reflect the real variety of political aspirations and give a voice in the processes of government to political interests and cultural identities currently not properly heard. It would propagate a much richer democratic culture and encourage far wider participation in political activity. It is only in such conditions of fermenting and maturing democracy that real socialist change can begin to be made.

The House of Commons should be reformed so that it can exercise proper control over the executive. This would include establishing properly effective select committees. Parliaments should also operate on a fixed-term basis, to eliminate the arbitrary power presently given to the sitting government. The House of Lords should be abolished.

The monarchy is anti-democratic and an anachronism. Any serious constitutional reform is bound to transform its position in the political system. In the long run, we assert our commitment to republicanism. In the short term there should be a limitation of its powers.

There should be a written constitution, including a bill of rights, which would define the rights and obligations of citizens with regard to the state and a proper division of powers between the various legislative bodies. Within such a bill of rights the special needs and rights of children should be recognised in line with the UN's Convention on the Rights of the Child.

There should be decentralised tiers of government at local, metropolitan, regional and national levels, with their powers enshrined in the constitution. This would include Scottish and Welsh parliaments. It might also include an English parliament, in which case Britain should move to a fully-fledged federal system.

A range of other democratic changes are needed. The police should be brought under local democratic control, the armed services reformed, the Special Branch abolished and state intelligence services made subject to select committee accountability. All state employees should enjoy proper democratic and union rights. Reform of the judiciary, magistrates' and coroners' courts should include rooting out racism and sexism, making appointment procedures accountable and modernising the processes of the law.

There should be a separation of religion from the state to help build a secular Britain in which there would be religious toleration, but not religious domination – by any religion or sect – for political ends. New laws would strengthen the existing race relations and anti-discrimination acts while abolishing those laws prejudicial to equal opportunity.

But beyond these constitutional changes there also needs to be a new kind of citizenship: one which combines universal rights with a recognition of difference and diversity, and thereby realises the goal of equal life chances.

We should be clear, however, that even an expanded concept of citizenship is limited, because it essentially defines the rights of individuals in relation to the state. There are other sources of power and inequality between individuals in society which can in some degree be regulated by the state but which also lie outside its sphere of operation.

An obvious example of this is gender inequality. Here the rights of one section of the population – women – are constrained by the power of another section – men. A more egalitarian relationship involves not only women gaining more rights, but also men giving up some of their privileges.

The reality of our society is that most of its life and activity take place outside the state. In our view a thriving civil society is the key to a pluralistic and vibrant polity and society. The state's role should not be one of policing civil society, or of paternalism, but an enabling role, one of partnership and co-operation.

conclusion

The undemocratic and deeply divisive radicalism of Thatcherism is now causing serious unease among an ever widening spectrum of the British people. The new times are producing and reproducing change at a revolutionary pace and on a scale which is turning all previous points of stability into the unrecognisable and the uncertain. In the search for new values and politics which can address this profound change, no single political party or movement has all the answers. However, a diversity of progressive traditions and streams of thought can be brought together to provide a spirit of cohesion around progressive change. They can provide a rich source for ideas to shape the new times to the interests of us all. This *Manifesto* has sought to shed light on how that can be achieved.